PRAYERS
FOR
ORDINARY
DAYS

PRAYERS FOR ORDINARY DAYS

HOWARD A. SNYDER

Cover design by Words2Live4
Page design by PerfecType, Nashville, Tennessee

Snyder, Howard A.
Prayers for ordinary days / Howard A. Snyder. – Frankin, Tennessee : Seedbed Publishing, ©2018.

pages ; cm.

ISBN 9781628243659 (paperback : alk. paper)
ISBN 9781628243666 (Mobi)
ISBN 9781628243673 (ePub)
ISBN 9781628243680 (uPDF) BS680.B8

1. Prayers. 2. Devotional calendars. I. Title.

BV245.S79 2018   242.8   2018939125

 Seedbed

SEEDBED PUBLISHING
Franklin, Tennessee
seedbed.com

For Marvelle Delorey Vannest,
and the many other friends and pray-ers
who kept insisting I must publish this book

CONTENTS

INTRODUCTION

HOW TO USE THIS BOOK

The longer we live the more sensible we should be of God's goodness to us in keeping us alive! And shall not the life thus kept by his providence, be devoted to his praise?

—John Wesley
Explanatory Notes upon the Old Testament,
commentary on Joshua 14:10

The apostle Paul wrote, "Not that I have already attained, or were already perfect, but I press on to reach the goal, because Christ Jesus has made me his own" (Phil. 3:12, author's paraphrase).

This book offers a year of prayers in that same spirit of aspiration, of pressing on in hope and in full confidence in God's unshakable promises.

Most of these prayers arose from private devotion. They were not written for other people, really. But as I began sharing my prayers on Facebook, people started asking for a book of prayers. Apparently, *my* prayer experience—my prayer aspirations—echoed in other folks' hearts. The reason, I think, is that our human needs are so basic and shared, regardless of age, gender, or culture. And because God's character and grace are so constant.

Maybe these prayers express the experience and aspirations of Christians globally, in many cultures, and through the ages. They breathe hope for the kingdom of God in fullness. They transcend nations and ethnicities, human philosophies, and political creeds. We lift our hearts in prayer to the God of the universe, the Lord sovereign over nations and nationalities, who is equally concerned with people everywhere, not just with our own nation or church or tribe.

Yet these prayers are deeply personal. Most arose from early-morning devotions. That is why some prayers refer to dawn or the morning hours. However, they can fruitfully be used any time of day, morning to night, or in hours of darkness.

Mostly these are prayers of praise, consecration, and intercession. Some, however, express confusion or vent frustration or anguish. Many arise out of questions, puzzles, even doubts. But deep down they are all *aspiring* prayers, praising God's goodness, asking his help, invoking his promises. As prayers of aspiration they are prayers of *respiration*—breathing in and out to God; God's Spirit responding with the Spirit's own inbreathing, stirring hope, courage, insight, and new strength.

Full-orbed prayer always includes praise and thanksgiving. Not all the prayers here express praise, however. Many are simply prayers of petition and intercession, like some of the Psalms. Such prayers do not embody the *totality* of a normal prayer life. The prayers in this book are no substitute for your own prayer and praise. Rather, they are supplements to help enrich your prayer life. They may serve as prayer starters, leading to fuller prayer and praise.

PRAYER RESOURCES

Books of prayers abound, as they have throughout Christian history. For millions of people in the English-speaking world, the classic volume is *The Book of Common Prayer* of the Anglican tradition. This gem is unsurpassed in depth, breadth, beauty, and literary quality. So I commend *The Book of Common Prayer*.

Other useful helps are the small *Field Guide for Daily Prayer* by Winfield Bevins, *Celtic Daily Prayer* from the Northumbria Community, and *Prayer: Finding the Heart's True Home* by Richard Foster. These last two books, in turn, list many other resources.

The small collection you have in your hands doesn't replace proven prayer resources, it just supplements them. Since these prayers arise mostly out of the late twentieth and early twenty-first centuries, they may speak particularly to people in today's world, even as we benefit from time-tested earlier resources. Because these prayers are mostly personal, you may find a depth of honesty and passion and concern and questioning, a mix of topics, and a comprehensiveness of scope not found in other prayer books.

With each prayer I include Scripture, a hymn excerpt, or a quotation from some other source. If no source is listed, the comment is my own.

Many of the prayers are paired with words from Psalms. Psalms has been called the prayer book of Jesus. It has become the prayer book of the church. No doubt many of the Psalms' prayers and phrases were often in Jesus' mind and heart as he communed with the Father in the Spirit.

King David was perhaps most a man after God's own heart (1 Sam. 13:14) when he prayed. We see this especially in the long Psalm 119. This psalm became one of my favorites once I realized that the psalm's many references to *law, statutes, commands,* and so forth, mean the whole biblical revelation of God's will, covenant, and gracious promises. In this psalm, to rejoice in God's law is to rejoice in all that God has revealed and all he promises to do—all his faithfulness to his covenant promises and his covenant people. So we rejoice and praise God's goodness.

A few of the prayers included here are quoted from other sources, as noted in each case. Some are adapted or paraphrased from *Daily Prayer* (compiled by Eric Milner-White and G. W. Briggs). In their original form these prayers are in the public domain.

GOD'S REIGN: "MAY YOUR WILL BE DONE ON EARTH!"

Jesus hears our prayers and prays through us by the Spirit. Jesus also showed us *how* to pray. His master model prayer was this: *May your kingdom come; may your will be done on earth as in heaven* (see Matthew 6:10; Luke 11:2). Jesus says this is how his followers should pray. Here is the grand goal. Many of the prayers in this book aim at this—that God's kingdom may come and his will be done fully on earth.

Behind the Lord's Prayer, and surely in Jesus' heart as he taught his disciples, was the full range of biblical promises of complete salvation, of creation healed, of the peaceable kingdom pictured so movingly in Isaiah 11 and similar passages. Passages such as these:

> The wolf shall live with the lamb, the leopard shall lie down with the kid, the calf and the lion and the fatling together, and a little child shall lead them. . . . They will not hurt or destroy on all my holy mountain; for the earth will be full of the knowledge of the LORD as the waters cover the sea. (Isa. 11:6, 9)

> The wilderness and the dry land shall be glad, the desert shall rejoice and blossom . . . Then the eyes of the blind shall be opened, and the ears of the deaf unstopped; then the lame shall leap like a deer, and the tongue of the speechless sing for joy. For waters shall break forth in the wilderness, and streams in the desert . . . And the ransomed of the LORD shall return, and come to Zion with singing; everlasting joy shall be upon their heads; they shall obtain joy and gladness, and sorrow and sighing shall flee away. (Isa. 35:1, 5–6, 10)

What the prophets foresaw; what Jesus began through his life, death, and resurrection; what the Bible still promises: this we pray for, intercede for, and seek to embody in our own lives and churches! To this end, the work of prayer and praise is indispensable.

Many prayer books don't include the entire created order and God's promises for its full healing in their scope of prayer. Often prayer books overlook the intimate biblical covenant relationship between God, humans, and the land or earth (see Genesis 9). The prayers I offer here aim to correct that oversight.

In my book *Salvation Means Creation Healed,* I show how the Bible is the story of God's covenant relationship *both* with people and with the land—the earth the Lord created. God's covenant is not solely with humans. This God–people–land covenant is basic for understanding the Bible, both the Old and the New Testaments.[1] The prayers in this book reflect this biblical holism. They invoke God's plan and promise to reconcile all creation; to bring all things in heaven and earth together, healed and restored, through Jesus Christ, as Scripture teaches (Eph. 1:10; Col. 1:19–20; Acts 3:18–21, and many other passages).

PRAYING IN COMMUNITY

Most of these prayers focus on personal, often private concerns. They are for private devotions. But a caution! These prayers assume you also participate in a praying Christian community—a group where prayers are shared, where you focus on each other's concerns and on God's redemptive mission in the world. We all need a believing, faithful Christian community or congregation to safeguard us from self-focused, private faith. The Christian faith is not "just me and

---

1. Howard A. Snyder with Joel Scandrett, *Salvation Means Creation Healed: The Ecology of Sin and Grace* (Eugene, OR: Cascade Books, 2011).

God." It concerns God's people throughout the earth and God's heart for the redemption of the world and the coming of his kingdom in fullness.

In terms of discipleship, this is not a stand-alone book. Your prayer life will benefit from other resources. I suggest you consider what God may say to you, for example, through *The Band Meeting: Rediscovering Relational Discipleship in Transformational Community* by Kevin Watson and Scott Kisker (Seedbed Publishing, 2017).

So use this collection of prayers to supplement, not replace, praying together with others. The healthiest Christian life is one where we pray and read the Bible in three ways: privately by ourselves, together in a small group, and corporately in the larger congregation.

USING THIS BOOK

For most Christians, Sunday is the primary day of worship and the real beginning of the week. For that reason we have formatted *Prayers for Ordinary Days* to help individuals cultivate a Sunday through Saturday prayer and meditation pattern. This book offers fifty-two complete weeks of daily prayers. If you start using this book on a day other than Sunday you can easily synchronize to the Sunday through Saturday schedule by using the additional prayers that begin on page 219.

Prayers for special days of the Christian year such as Advent, Christmas, Good Friday, Easter, and Pentecost are also included. Use these prayers at the appropriate season of the year, if you wish, either in addition to or in place of the prayer for that particular day. Note that since the traditional Christian year begins with Advent, four weeks before Christmas, it starts several weeks before the calendar year.

I have also included a dozen additional prayers for special situations or circumstances, such as a birthday, a time of sorrow or depression, or a special time of thanksgiving.

Communing with God is very personal. We must all find our own daily pattern within the great tradition of the Christian faith. Here is what works for me: first I pray with Isaiah, "Holy, holy, holy is the LORD of hosts; the whole earth is full of his glory" (Isa. 6:3). Then I read my own daily prayer. God often uses this to speak to my heart. Or maybe I'll write a new prayer. I then go on to my other praises, prayers, and intercessions, following a weekly pattern I have developed over years. You will already have, or will develop, your own pattern that works for you, using such resources as you personally find helpful or are recommended by your church community.

SPECIAL NOTE ON GOD LANGUAGE

Words we use are symbols or signs pointing to something else. The word "chair" is not itself a chair; it's the five-letter word we use to designate what we understand to be a chair.

This simple truth gets complicated when we talk about God! The Bible speaks of God as "rock," "fortress," "shield," "fire." Scripture is a vast storehouse of metaphors and word pictures. So also with many hymns. We are used to this, so usually we don't think much about it.

In this book I use familiar metaphors or images of God. Sometimes, however, I find it helpful to use less traditional metaphors. For example, in a few prayers I refer to God as Mother. I do this partly because the Bible itself uses maternal images for God. For example, "As a mother comforts her child, so I will comfort you" (Isa. 66:13). Such images remind us that God shows qualities and characteristics we typically view as feminine, as well as qualities we think of as masculine. In fact, what is *masculine* or *feminine* and what is *paternal* or *maternal* varies from culture to culture. God the Holy Trinity is Lord of all cultures, however.

Maternal imagery for God is common in some Christian traditions, though relatively rare among Protestants. Some users of this book may find such language troublesome or unhelpful. If this is so with you, just skip the prayer for now. Use instead one of the extra prayers at the end of the book. You may later want to return to the prayer—perhaps after finishing the complete cycle. God's Spirit may now freshly speak to you through this prayer.

I pray the Holy Spirit may use these simple prayers in your life, weaving them into the complex ecology of his kingdom purposes to spark renewal, revival, awakening, and reform—not only in your own personal life, but also in the wide world until God's kingdom comes in perfect, peaceable fullness.

PRAYERS
FOR
ORDINARY
DAYS

WEEK ONE

SUNDAY

Lord God, as this day dawns, I praise you and thank you for all your works. Holy Lord, I worship you and glory in your goodness and truth and justice. Dear Lord, manifest Jesus in my life today through the power of your Spirit, I pray. May this be a day of rest and worship as I trust my way into your care and trust fully in your good promises. Glory be to you, Lord Most High, Precious Savior. Amen.

O sing to the LORD a new song;
    sing to the LORD, all the earth.
Sing to the LORD, bless his name;
    tell of his salvation from day to day.
Declare his glory among the nations,
    his marvelous works among all the peoples.
                  —Psalm 96:1–3

MONDAY

I come before you at this moment, O God, remembering that many thousands of your children are also bowing before you and calling on your aid right now throughout the earth. In gratitude before you I remember that many people daily are praying for me. Surrounded by this "great cloud of witnesses," and trusting in the intercession of Jesus on my behalf, I give myself anew to you for this day and week, with peace and joy. Amen.

�֍ ✳ ✳

Therefore, since we are surrounded by so great a cloud of witnesses, let us lay aside every weight and the sin that clings so closely, and let us run with perseverance the race that is set before us, looking to Jesus the pioneer and perfecter of our faith, who for the sake of the joy that was set before him endured the cross, disregarding its shame, and has taken his seat at the right hand of the throne of God.

—Hebrews 12:1–2

TUESDAY

Precious Jesus, you are indispensable to me! I cannot live without you. Yet in my weakness I sometimes fail to follow you closely. Strengthen my will, warm my heart, and enlighten my mind, that I may do your perfect will today. Sustain and guide me by your inward Spirit until I rest in sleep this night. Amen.

✳ ✳ ✳

God is on your side, honestly more than you are on your own.
—Richard Rohr with Mike Morrell
The Divine Dance: The Trinity and Your Transformation

WEDNESDAY

Sovereign Lord, at this midpoint in the week I renew my covenant with you, undisturbed by my weakness because my confidence is in your mercy and strength. All praise to you for your tender lovingkindness. Grant me the peace to rest in you and to walk calmly in the steps of Jesus through every hour of this day, I pray. Amen.

Say among the nations, "The LORD is king!
   The world is firmly established; it shall never be moved.
   He will judge the peoples with equity."

—Psalm 96:10

THURSDAY

Lord Jesus, who laid down your life for the sins of the world and the healing of creation, hear now my quiet prayer. I gladly give myself to you at the beginning of this day. May the healing, life-giving love, and power shown in your death and life be my power to live faithfully for you today, I pray. Amen.

Let the heavens be glad, and let the earth rejoice;
   let the sea roar, and all that fills it;
   let the field exult, and everything in it.
Then shall all the trees of the forest sing for joy
   before the LORD; for he is coming,
   for he is coming to judge the earth.
He will judge the world with righteousness,
   and the peoples with his truth.

—Psalm 96:11–13

FRIDAY

Lord, another week draws to a close. I have walked with you in peace and you have been my Guide. Sanctify every good intention and act as a sacrament toward greater faithfulness. Forgive my sins and failures, and strengthen me by your Spirit to walk faithfully before you today. May I be Jesus Christ to some needy child of yours before this day ends. Amen.

So acknowledge today and take to heart that the LORD is God in heaven above and on the earth beneath; there is no other. Keep his statutes and his commandments, which I am commanding you today for your own well-being and that of your descendants after you, so that you may long remain in the land that the LORD your God is giving you for all time.

—Deuteronomy 4:39–40

SATURDAY

Lord, this is your day, your world, and I am your servant. Thank you for the assurance this day that you are King of Kings and Lord of Lords, and that in the fullness of time the kingdom of this world is becoming the kingdom of Jesus Christ. I submit to your sovereign lordship today, with joy in the unshakable assurance of your victory. Amen.

O come, let us worship and bow down:
   let us kneel before the LORD our maker.
For he is our God;
   and we are the people of his pasture,
   and the sheep of his hand.

—Psalm 95:6–7 KJV

WEEK TWO

SUNDAY

Thank you, Sovereign Lord, for your rest! I praise and worship you for granting rest to your people, and even more for the greater rest that yet remains for the people of God. May I rest fully in your peace today, and may I trust wholly in your promise of final, perfect Sabbath. Amen.

❋ ❋ ❋

> Every joy or trial falleth from above,
> Traced upon our dial by the Sun of Love;
> We may trust Him fully, all for us to do;
> They who trust Him wholly find Him wholly true.
> —Frances Ridley Havergal,
> "Like a River Glorious," 1876

MONDAY

Lord God, Father, Son, and Holy Spirit, I worship you at the beginning of this day. My heart is full of praise and gratitude to you as I long for the full coming of your kingdom in the world and in my life. Gracious, loving Father, guide and keep me this day, that I may live for your honor and praise, I pray. Amen.

Blessed be the LORD, the God of Israel,
    who alone does wondrous things.
Blessed be his glorious name forever;
    may his glory fill the whole earth.
Amen and Amen.

—Psalm 72:18–19

TUESDAY

For the beauty of the earth, for the vastness of the skies, for your great love and wisdom shown in all you have made, O Lord, I give you joyful praise. Glory and honor be yours, great God, I pray, throughout your creation, in the heavenlies, and in my life today. Amen.

For as the earth brings forth its shoots,
    and as a garden causes what is sown in it to spring up,
so the Lord GOD will cause righteousness and praise
    to spring up before all the nations.

—Isaiah 61:11

WEDNESDAY

Lord of life, who raised Jesus Christ from the dead, I thank you for the promise of resurrection. Thank you for life here and hereafter. Life-giving Spirit, so deepen your life in me today that the true promise of life in Jesus may be seen by all. Keep me in you throughout and beyond this present life, that I may dwell in the house of the Lord forever. Amen.

Christ has been raised from the dead, the first fruits of those who have died. For since death came through a human being, the resurrection of the dead has also come through a human being; for as all die in Adam, so all will be made alive in Christ. But each in his own order: Christ the first fruits, then at his coming those who belong to Christ.

—1 Corinthians 15:20–23

THURSDAY

O Jesus, you who bring light to the nations and salvation to the whole earth, I bow before you in awe and worship this day. Loving Savior, praise be to you. Thank you for your saving, guiding work in my life. Help me to walk in your ways and purposes this day, I pray. Amen.

* * *

"For so the Lord has commanded us, saying,

> 'I have set you to be a light for the Gentiles,
> so that you may bring salvation to the ends of the earth.'"

When the Gentiles heard this, they were glad and praised the word of the Lord; and as many as had been destined for eternal life became believers.

—Acts 13:47–48

FRIDAY

O God, Blessed Savior, I thank you for your presence in my life and your work in my heart. Help me, O God, not to be so focused on your interior presence that I fail to live a righteous and just life for the sake of your kingdom in the world around me. Make me a true witness of your kingdom in every dimension of life, without compromise, I pray. Amen.

✴ ✴ ✴

> Sing praises to the LORD, O you his faithful ones,
>   and give thanks to his holy name.
> For his anger is but for a moment;
>   his favor is for a lifetime.
> Weeping may linger for the night,
>   but joy comes with the morning.

—Psalm 30:4–5

SATURDAY

Gentle Savior, full of love and compassion, I worship you and commit my way today into your caring hands. Blessed Holy Spirit, keep me in your peace and presence today, I pray. Glory and praise be to you, loving Father. Holy Lord, be my life and joy and peace this day, I pray. Amen.

✴ ✴ ✴

> I will bless the LORD at all times;
>   his praise shall continually be in
>   my mouth.
> My soul makes its boast in the LORD;
>   let the humble hear and be glad.
> O magnify the LORD with me,
>   and let us exalt his name together.
>
> I sought the LORD, and he answered me,
>   and delivered me from all my fears.
> Look to him, and be radiant;
>   so your faces shall never be ashamed.

—Psalm 34:1–5

WEEK THREE

SUNDAY

O God, who pours out your Spirit for the common good, pour your Spirit anew into my life today, and on your church, I pray. Lord Jesus, live in me daily by your Spirit, as you work to renew the face of the earth. Amen.

❋ ❋ ❋

O taste and see that the LORD is good;
  happy are those who take refuge in him.
                                        —Psalm 34:8

MONDAY

Loving, Holy God, I worship you and affirm that you do all things well. Yet I see so much suffering, oppression, and disorder in the world and wonder why your kingdom and *shalom* do not come more quickly. Lord God, I trust you and hope in you. Work in my life today that I may be a sign that you *are* love and you *are* working in the world even now. I pray through Jesus Christ, the Prince of Peace. Amen.

> "Talk no more so very proudly,
>   let not arrogance come from your mouth;
> for the LORD is a God of knowledge,
>   and by him actions are weighed."
>
> —1 Samuel 2:3

TUESDAY

Spirit of God, breath of life and joy and renewal, I praise you and rejoice in your presence and promise this day. Lord God, fill me with your life today that, like Jesus, I may truly walk in the Spirit as I walk in the world. Dear Lord, be my life and my joy and my guide, I pray. Amen.

> Be glad in the LORD and rejoice, O righteous,
>   and shout for joy, all you upright in heart.
>
> —Psalm 32:11

WEDNESDAY

Holy Lord, Father of all comfort, I worship you and rest in your peace. I commit my way to you for this day. As I direct my attention to many things, Lord, may I be led by your Spirit and be a channel of your grace to others. Glory be to you, Blessed Lord, Savior, Healer. Amen.

* * *

Come, O children, listen to me;
  I will teach you the fear of the LORD.
Which of you desires life,
  and covets many days to enjoy good?
Keep your tongue from evil,
  and your lips from speaking deceit.
Depart from evil, and do good;
  seek peace, and pursue it.

—Psalm 34:11–14

THURSDAY

Thank you, O God, for your church, the body of Christ. Lord Jesus, thank you for forming your community of worship, witness, and discipleship. Blessed Holy Spirit, renew and work through your church today, I pray, and through me, for the full revealing of the kingdom of God. I pray through Jesus Christ, Lord and King and Healer. Amen.

* * *

"Do not be afraid, little flock, for your Father delights to give you the kingdom."

—Luke 12:32 (author's paraphrase)

FRIDAY

God of grace and wisdom, I lay my way this day in your strong hands. Thank you for the night's rest and the joy of serving. Lord Jesus, guide me by your Spirit today; help me walk in your ways; may I do faithfully the work you have given me. Praise and honor be to you, Holy Trinity. Amen.

✻ ✻ ✻

The LORD is near to the brokenhearted,
  and saves the crushed in spirit.

Many are the afflictions of the righteous,
  but the LORD rescues them from them all.
  —Psalm 34:18–19

SATURDAY

Holy Trinity, God of grace and wisdom, I give you thanks that Jesus came into the world as a servant, not to be served but to serve, and to open the way to life for all. Blessed Savior, fill me with your Spirit of compassion today, that I may be a loving servant of Jesus and of those who suffer and those who quest, to the glory of your name and the revealing of your kingdom, I pray. Amen.

✻ ✻ ✻

"[W]hoever wishes to be great among you must be your servant, and whoever wishes to be first among you must be your slave; just as the Son of Man came not to be served but to serve, and to give his life a ransom for many."

—Jesus (Matthew 20:26–28)

WEEK FOUR

Sunday

Jesus, Savior, who came to seek and save the lost and spread the good news of God's reign, I worship you in praise and joy. Blessed Jesus, guide me today by your Holy Spirit that I may see as you would have me see, think as you would have me think, and do as you would have me do. To the praise of the Father, I pray. Amen.

The LORD redeems the life of his servants:
none of those who trust in him shall be desolate.
—Psalm 34:22 KJV (author's paraphrase)

MONDAY

Dear Father, Creator of all, I worship you in your glory and wondrous energy. Blessed Jesus, Lord and Savior, I praise your life and death for all of creation. Holy Spirit, Guide and Witness, I praise your work today in drawing people to yourself and renewing the face of the earth. Blessed Trinity, I worship you and give my life in service to your kingdom this day. Amen.

✳ ✳ ✳

"Only fear the LORD, and serve him faithfully with all your heart; for consider what great things he has done for you."

—1 Samuel 12:24

TUESDAY

Holy Lord, loving Savior, Spirit of truth and justice, I worship you and bow in adoration as another day begins. My hope and my expectation for the full coming of your kingdom are lodged in you. Holy Lord, breathe your presence newly into my life today, and may Jesus Christ be honored in all I do and say. I pray to the glory of Father, Son, and Holy Spirit. Amen.

✳ ✳ ✳

"[I]t may be that the LORD will act for us; for nothing can hinder the LORD from saving by many or by few."

—1 Samuel 14:6

WEDNESDAY

Praise be to you this day, O Lord, Holy Father, Son, and Spirit. Glory and honor I give you. I open my heart to love you and my eyes to see you and your works this day. Holy Trinity, stir my heart to worship and serve you in joy and faithfulness, I pray through Jesus Christ our Lord. Amen.

✶ ✶ ✶

O Lord, all my longing is known to you;
my sighing is not hidden from you.
—Psalm 38:9

THURSDAY

O God of grace and glory, I worship you today and open my mind and spirit to you and your love. Holy, loving God, all praise and honor be to you! By your loving Spirit, work transformingly in my life today, that my motives may be pure, my love sincere, and my actions consistent with your kingdom purposes, I pray. Amen.

✶ ✶ ✶

Create in me a clean heart, O God,
and put a new and right spirit within me.
Do not cast me away from your presence,
and do not take your holy spirit from me.
Restore to me the joy of your salvation,
and sustain in me a willing spirit.
—Psalm 51:10–12

FRIDAY

Praise be to you, O Lord. Holy Spirit of God, help me this day be more like Jesus, I pray. Heavenly Father, breathe into me this day your loving Spirit; form Jesus in me, that I may reflect Jesus and his kingdom in all my inward thoughts and outward acts, I ask through your mercy. Amen.

Do not forsake me, O LORD;
O my God, do not be far from me;
make haste to help me,
O Lord, my salvation.
—Psalm 38:21–22

SATURDAY

O Sovereign Lord, morning, noon, and evening, and when I awake in the nighttime hours, my prayer and my song is: may your kingdom come and your will be done on earth as in heaven. O God, may your kingdom come. Holy Spirit, use me this day for your kingdom purposes, to the praise and glory of Jesus Christ, I pray. Amen.

❋ ❋ ❋

By day the LORD commands his steadfast love,
and at night his song is with me,
a prayer to the God of my life.
—Psalm 42:8

WEEK FIVE

SUNDAY

Waking or sleeping, O God, I thank you that I am in your care. Holy Lord, I rest in you today, putting all my trust and hope in you and depending on the work of your Spirit to sustain me and to make Jesus real in my life. Holy Trinity, be in and around, behind, and before me this day, I pray, as I worship and serve you. Amen.

❈ ❈ ❈

"And now, O Lord, what do I wait for?
    My hope is in you."

—Psalm 39:7

MONDAY

O God, I worship you this day and long to know you more deeply. Show me your ways! Though your ways are not the ways of humankind, I ask that by your Spirit you will reveal your ways more fully to my soul, that I may faithfully and fruitfully serve your purposes. I honor and praise you, Lord Jesus, this day. I pray that *my* ways may become *your* ways. Amen.

[Moses prayed to the Lord,] "If I have found favor in your sight, show me your ways, so that I may know you and find favor in your sight. . . ." [The Lord] said, "My presence will go with you, and I will give you rest."

—Exodus 33:13–14

TUESDAY

Lord God, wise guide and Sovereign Spirit, I worship you and bow in submission before you. O God, I will to do your will in all things. Work in me by your Spirit today, I pray, that my intentions may be pure and my will may be strong to do your will; to follow in the way of Jesus. Amen.

You desire truth in the inward being;
therefore teach me wisdom in my secret heart.
—Psalm 51:6

WEDNESDAY

O God, you promise to provide everything your people need for life and godliness and kingdom witness. As you tell us to pray without ceasing, I ask that today you may be in all my thoughts and intents and meditations, that this day may be a day of unceasing prayer to you. Holy Spirit, draw me repeatedly to you, and may my heart be at deep rest in constant application to you. In the name of Jesus, I pray. Amen.

Rejoice evermore. Pray without ceasing. In every thing give thanks: for this is the will of God in Christ Jesus concerning you.

—1 Thessalonians 5:16–18 KJV

THURSDAY

O God, I thank you that through your grace, repentance and forgiveness of sins is preached to the nations. Thank you for the loving, atoning work of Jesus Christ for all people. I trust in you today, Lord, and seek to help spread your good news. Praise, honor, and glory be to you, Blessed Trinity. Amen.

"Thus it is written, that the Messiah is to suffer and to rise from the dead on the third day, and that repentance and forgiveness of sins is to be proclaimed in his name to all nations, beginning from Jerusalem."

—Jesus (Luke 24:46–47)

FRIDAY

Lord God, high and holy yet near and loving, I honor and glorify you this day. Praise be to you, Father, Son, and Holy Spirit. I rejoice in your being, your truth, your self-giving, and your plan for the ages. Holy Spirit, fill and use me this day, to the manifestation and praise of Jesus, I pray. Amen.

> O send out your light and your truth;
>   let them lead me;
> let them bring me to your holy hill
>   and to your dwelling.

—Psalm 43:3

SATURDAY

O God, I want to be alive to your power and all your good purposes today, and dead to all that would lead me away from you or stain my commitment to you. Blessed Holy Spirit, live in and through me today, I pray, that Jesus Christ may be the center and focus of all I say, do, or think. I pray through Jesus Christ my Lord. Amen.

We know that Christ, being raised from the dead, will never die again; death no longer has dominion over him. The death he died, he died to sin, once for all; but the life he lives, he lives to God. So you also must consider yourselves dead to sin and alive to God in Christ Jesus.

—Romans 6:9–11

WEEK SIX

SUNDAY

Holy Spirit, as you have given a rich diversity of spiritual gifts to your church, I pray you will build your community in love and effective ministry through your power and the richness of your gifts. Gracious Spirit, work in and through my life today, that the gifts you have given me may nourish the health of the body and the extension of Christ's kingdom, I pray. Amen.

✳ ✳ ✳

Now there are varieties of gifts, but the same Spirit; and there are varieties of services, but the same Lord; and there are varieties of activities, but it is the same God who activates all of them in everyone. To each is given the manifestation of the Spirit for the common good.

—1 Corinthians 12:4–7

MONDAY

Holy Trinity, life and giver of life, I worship you and praise your holy name. Lord God, I humbly ask that you would grant me in some small leavening measure the energy of the Father, the compassion of the Son, and the discernment of the Holy Spirit, that my life this day may reflect your glory. Amen.

❄ ❄ ❄

> In God we have boasted continually,
> and we will give thanks to your name forever.
> —Psalm 44:8

TUESDAY

Gracious, clever, long-seeing God, I worship you with all my being. Glory be to you, Lord Most High. I set you before me and all else behind me just now, willing to serve you this day in the energy of your Spirit. Lord, give me more and more of a passion for your purposes, I pray. Amen.

❄ ❄ ❄

> Your throne, O God, endures forever and ever.
> Your royal scepter is a scepter of equity.
> —Psalm 45:6

WEDNESDAY

Lord God, loving Savior, I rejoice today in your wonderful grace. As I begin this day surrounded by the "great cloud of witnesses" in heaven and on earth, give me a lively sense of running the race before the immense audience of your saints and martyrs who have gone before. Keep me strong and faithful in the race today, I pray. Amen.

Whom have I in heaven but you?
    And there is nothing on earth that I desire other than you.
My flesh and my heart may fail,
    but God is the strength of my heart and my portion forever.
                                                    —Psalm 73:25–26

THURSDAY

Lord of the universe, loving God, I worship you today for your sovereign power and limitless goodness. All your works praise you, O Lord, and I join my voice in praise. May I walk constantly in your joy and rest fully in your good providence and wise provision this day, I pray. Amen.

"The more we see of God's glory in his works, the more we desire to see. And the more we are affected with what we have seen of God, the better we are prepared for farther discoveries."

                            —John Wesley, commentary on Deuteronomy 3:24
                            Explanatory Notes upon the Old Testament

FRIDAY

Blessed Jesus, Lord Most High, I worship you today! All praise, honor, and glory be yours. As I live my life at this intersection of space and time, spirit and matter, now and forever, may I honor you and find in you my true life. Be God Most Nigh as I walk with you today, I pray. Amen.

✳ ✳ ✳

For thus says the high and lofty one
    who inhabits eternity, whose name is Holy:
I dwell in the high and holy place,
    and also with those who are contrite and humble in spirit,
to revive the spirit of the humble,
    and to revive the heart of the contrite.

—Isaiah 57:15

SATURDAY

Lamb of God, who takes away the sin of the world, I worship you now in quiet awe. Praise, honor, and glory be yours. Thank you for giving yourself for me and for all your broken creation. By your Holy Spirit inspire me to live today "the life laid down," I pray, to the glory of God the Father. Amen.

✳ ✳ ✳

The next day [John the Baptist] saw Jesus coming toward him and declared, "Here is the Lamb of God who takes away the sin of the world!"

—John 1:29

WEEK SEVEN

SUNDAY

Lord Jesus, in whom all things visible and invisible cohere, I bow in awe and reverence before you at the beginning of this day of rest. O Savior, worthy of all praise and honor, bend to listen and lift me today as I lay my life before you and rest in your peace. Praise be to you, Lord Christ! Amen.

❋ ❋ ❋

[Jesus Christ] is the image of the invisible God, the firstborn of all creation; for in him all things in heaven and on earth were created, things visible and invisible, whether thrones or dominions or rulers or powers—all things have been created through him and for him. He himself is before all things, and in him all things hold together.

—Colossians 1:15–17

Monday

Merciful God, Mother of Love, Father of Light, I give myself newly to you this day. All praise, honor, and glory be yours, Sovereign Lord. I accept this week with its possibilities and challenges as a fresh gift from your bounty. Help me to walk with you daily as a loving child of the light. Amen.

Blessed be the God and Father of our Lord Jesus Christ, the Father of mercies and the God of all consolation, who consoles us in all our affliction, so that we may be able to console those who are in any affliction with the consolation with which we ourselves are consoled by God.

—2 Corinthians 1:3–4

Tuesday

All praise and honor be yours, Eternal Father, God of truth and love. As I bow humbly before you, fill me with your loving Spirit, I pray. Let me be today as Jesus was—no more concerned about the things of this world than he was, yet just as concerned about the things of this world as he was and is. Live your life in and through me this day, loving Savior. Amen.

Therefore, since we are receiving a kingdom that cannot be shaken, let us give thanks, by which we offer to God an acceptable worship with reverence and awe; for indeed our God is a consuming fire.

—Hebrews 12:28–29

WEDNESDAY

Holy, Holy, Holy Lord, Blessed Trinity! You are threefold love, and your love shown through Jesus Christ has conquered death and evil. O God, strengthen my faith-grip on the reality of your victory and the power of your love—past, present, and future. May I walk boldly in your love today, I pray. Amen.

"Be still, and know that I am God!
  I am exalted among the nations,
  I am exalted in the earth."
The LORD of hosts is with us;
  the God of Jacob is our refuge.
                    —Psalm 46:10–11

THURSDAY

Lord Jesus, gentle Savior, I rest today in your embrace. I worship you, my Lord and my God—Way, Truth, Life! Let this sacred moment sanctify every moment of the day. Keep my spirit deeply at rest in you through all this day's busyness, as I abide calmly and quietly in your peace. Amen.

Sing praises to God, sing praises:
  sing praises unto our King, sing praises.
For God is the King of all the earth:
  sing ye praises with understanding.
                    —Psalm 47:6–7 KJV

FRIDAY

O God of truth, all-knowing, I bow in quiet worship before you. Lord Jesus, you know that I often intend better than I do. By your Holy Spirit, help me this day to translate good intention into strong will and holy action, I pray. I worship you, my hope and the source of my power to live. Praise be to you, Holy Trinity. Amen.

I waited patiently for the LORD;
  he inclined to me and heard my cry. . . .
He put a new song in my mouth,
  a song of praise to our God.
Many will see and fear,
  and put their trust in the LORD.
—Psalm 40:1, 3

SATURDAY

Holy, Holy, Holy Lord!—before all time, yet all time filling; beyond comprehension, yet comprehensible in Jesus Christ. Praise, honor, glory, and the joyful worship of all creation be yours this day, Sovereign One. I praise you that you are love! Live your holy love in and through me today, I pray. Amen.

We ponder your steadfast love, O God,
  in the midst of your temple.
Your name, O God, like your praise,
  reaches to the ends of the earth.
Your right hand is filled with victory.
—Psalm 48:9–10

WEEK EIGHT

SUNDAY

Gracious Lord, Blessed Trinity, I worship you today in the wonder and beauty of your tri-unity. Blessed and holy are you, Father, Son, and loving Spirit. I give myself freely to you and rest now in your peace. May I walk in unity with you and in community with your children this day, I pray. Amen.

❈ ❈ ❈

> O Lord, open my lips,
>   and my mouth will declare your praise.
>   —Psalm 51:15

MONDAY

O God, Sovereign Lord, I bow before you now and worship you with all my being. May the respiration of my body and soul keep rhythm today with the pulses of your Spirit. May your breeze blow fresh, lovely, healing truth, and may I move with your currents, I pray. Amen.

Yours is the day, yours also the night;
  you established the luminaries and the sun.
You have fixed all the bounds of the earth;
  you made summer and winter.

—Psalm 74:16–17

TUESDAY

I praise and honor you today, Lord Christ! Through the years of my life you have been my God, my joy, my strength. In this new day, may I not stray from your path but walk before you in holiness and righteousness. Be glorified in my life today, I pray. Amen.

Yours is the day, yours also the night;

At the set time that I appoint
  I will judge with equity.
When the earth totters, with all its inhabitants,
  it is I who keep its pillars steady.

—Psalm 75:2–3

WEDNESDAY

O Lord, Eternal God, I join all your works in praising you this day. Spirit of creation and new creation, I worship you in awe and hope, resting in your present and yearning for your future. Live in me always, and may I be open to your new work in me and in your world today, I pray through Jesus Christ, the Risen One. Amen.

You have multiplied, O Lord my God,
   your wondrous deeds and your thoughts toward us;
   none can compare with you.
Were I to proclaim and tell of them,
   they would be more than can be counted.

—Psalm 40:5

THURSDAY

O God, I come to you at the beginning of this day confessing my weakness and claiming your strength. I thank you for your Word that your strength is made perfect in our weakness. All praise, glory, and honor be to you, Father/Mother God, Jesus Christ King and Redeemer, and Holy Spirit, my Helper and Guide. Lead me by the hand through all the paths of this day, I pray. Amen.

[The Lord] said to me, "My grace is sufficient for you, for power is made perfect in weakness." So, I will boast all the more gladly of my weaknesses, so that the power of Christ may dwell in me.

—2 Corinthians 12:9

FRIDAY

God of the universe, high over all, I bow in humble worship before you in this quiet time and place. I honor you; I acknowledge none beside you, Triune God. Let me by your Spirit live today the Jesus-life, I pray, and join all creation in praising you. Amen.

✳ ✳ ✳

> Glorious are you, more majestic
> than the everlasting mountains.
> —Psalm 76:4

SATURDAY

With the march of days and seasons, O God, you remain Lord and Sovereign, Reconciler, Healer, and loving Sustainer. I worship you, who hold times and seasons in your hands and fully intend to fulfill all your good purposes. Help me this day to discern your timing and follow your way, I pray. Amen.

✳ ✳ ✳

> I will call to mind the deeds of the LORD;
> I will remember your wonders of old.
> I will meditate on all your work,
> and muse on your mighty deeds.
> Your way, O God, is holy.
> What god is so great as our God?
> You are the God who works wonders;
> you have displayed your might among the peoples.
> —Psalm 77:11–14

WEEK NINE

SUNDAY

O God, Lord of the ages, I worship you in reverent wonder. I thank you that you have the whole world in your hands. As time flows into eternity, may I be deeply conscious of the truly important things. Help me live this day as Jesus did, filled with a Spirit-led sense of priorities. Amen.

✻ ✻ ✻

Be pleased, O LORD, to deliver me:
O LORD, make haste to help me.
—Psalm 40:13 KJV

MONDAY

Dear Lord, you have made birds and trees, flowers and mountains, strange creatures large and small. How great and imaginative are your works! I wonder and joy in all you have made, and that you made and love me. Help me to walk faithfully in your world today, with eyes wide open, I pray. Amen.

✻ ✻ ✻

Bless the LORD, O my soul.
   O LORD my God, you are very great.
You are clothed with honor and majesty,
   wrapped in light as with a garment.
You stretch out the heavens like a tent,
   you set the beams of your chambers
     on the waters,
you make the clouds your chariot,

you ride on the wings of the wind,
   you make the winds your messengers,
   fire and flame your ministers.

You set the earth on its foundations,
   so that it shall never be shaken.
         —Psalm 104:1–5

TUESDAY

"As a mother comforts her child, so I will comfort you," says the Lord. I come to you now needing your comfort and your warm, loving arms. Thank you for nursing me as I have grown to love you more and more. Fill me today with the same love that flows to all you have made and all you care for, I pray. Amen.

✻ ✻ ✻

As a mother comforts her child,
   so I will comfort you;
   you shall be comforted in Jerusalem.
         —Isaiah 66:13

WEDNESDAY

O God, I look at the stars and am reminded of vastness. How great you are! I honor you and ask that you would plant deep within me today a sense of your greatness and power and glory, all bound up in love. Praise be to you, Holy Trinity! Amen.

❋ ❋ ❋

God made the two great lights—the greater light to rule the day and the lesser light to rule the night—and the stars. God set them in the dome of the sky to give light upon the earth, to rule over the day and over the night, and to separate the light from the darkness. And God saw that it was good.

—Genesis 1:16–18

THURSDAY

Lord Jesus, thank you for giving your life for the life of the world. I trust in your atonement, and ask that its effects would be spread through all my life today, for the health and salvation of others, and the healing of your world. Amen.

❋ ❋ ❋

The love of Christ urges us on, because we are convinced that one has died for all; therefore all have died. And he died for all, so that those who live might live no longer for themselves, but for him who died and was raised for them.

—2 Corinthians 5:14–15

FRIDAY

O Lord, you alone are God! At the beginning of this beautiful day, filled with your grace, I worship you and exalt your holy name. Walk with me today as I seek to walk with you, Lord Jesus, I pray, by your Holy Spirit. Amen.

[W]e will tell to the coming generation
the glorious deeds of the LORD, and his might,
and the wonders that he has done. . . .
that the next generation might know them,
the children yet unborn,
and rise up and tell them to their children,
so that they should set their hope in God,
and not forget the works of God,
but keep his commandments.

—Psalm 78:4, 6–7

SATURDAY

O Gracious One, loving Lord, I bow in awe and joy before you this day. I rejoice that your love extends to all you have made, and that you seek and save the lost. Give me today grace and vision to serve your mission, I pray. Amen.

Restore us, O God of hosts;
let your face shine, that we may be saved. . . .
Then we will never turn back from you;
give us life, and we will call on your name.

—Psalm 80:7, 18

SUNDAY

Blessed Holy Spirit, who still breathes and broods over all your creation, hear my prayer. I give myself to you in service to Jesus. Fill me now and live in and through me today, I pray, Lord Most High. Amen.

> How lovely is your dwelling place,
>   O LORD of hosts!
> My soul longs, indeed it faints
>   for the courts of the LORD;
> my heart and my flesh sing for joy
>   to the living God.
>
> —Psalm 84:1–2

MONDAY

O Lord, you are God, from everlasting to everlasting. Here I am at this small dot in time. Thank you for your love for me! Guide me this day, and prepare me to share your love-filled eternity, I pray. Amen.

> The LORD God is a sun and shield;
>   he bestows favor and honor.
> No good thing does the LORD withhold
>   from those who walk uprightly.
> O LORD of hosts,
>   happy is everyone who trusts in you.
>   —Psalm 84:11–12

TUESDAY

Lord Jesus, you are the Way of Life. Help me today to *walk* with you. Order my steps; help me guard my heart for you alone; and keep me in your path to the end, I pray. Amen.

The LORD said to Samuel, "Do not look on his appearance or on the height of his stature, because I have rejected him; for the LORD does not see as mortals see; they look on the outward appearance, but the LORD looks on the heart."

                     —1 Samuel 16:7

WEDNESDAY

Lord God, I worship you today. I will to be governed by your sovereign will. I acknowledge your power, your authority, and your good, gracious interest in all things. Holy Spirit, help me walk in joyful obedience this day, I pray. Amen.

Will you not revive us again,
    so that your people may rejoice in you?
Show us your steadfast love, O LORD,
    and grant us your salvation.

—Psalm 85:6–7

THURSDAY

Dear Father, you tell me that "I can do all things through [Christ] who strengthens me" (Phil. 4:13). I believe and claim this truth in my life today. By your Spirit, direct me surely in the things you would have me do now to your glory. I pray through Jesus Christ. Amen.

Let me hear what God the LORD will speak,
    for he will speak peace to his people,
    to his faithful, to those who turn to him in their hearts.
Surely his salvation is at hand for those who fear him,
    that his glory may dwell in our land.

—Psalm 85:8–9

FRIDAY

Holy Lord, Maker and Sustainer and Renewer of all things, I worship you. Here in this small spot of space and time, my thoughts expand into space, beyond earth, beyond time and place, in wonder at your creation and your glory and vast wisdom and love. Praise and honor be yours, Holy Lord, now and in all the unknowable dimensions of your glory and your good, provident purposes. Hold me firmly in your love today, in time and beyond time, I pray. Amen.

Sing aloud to God our strength;
    shout for joy to the God of Jacob.
Raise a song, sound the tambourine,
    the sweet lyre with the harp.
—Psalm 81:1–2

SATURDAY

Blessed Holy Spirit, breath of God, I thank you that you still hover and breathe over the world you made. I praise and honor you today. Fill me anew with your grace that I may discern and follow your movement, I pray. Amen.

"Call on me in the day of trouble;
    I will deliver you, and you shall glorify me."
—Psalm 50:15

SUNDAY

O Holy Lord, our Father and Mother, thank you for your love and care. By your Spirit, please help those who once knew you but have wandered away to discover anew the simplicity of the gospel and the reality of Jesus—to learn that, indeed, God is love. I pray in the name of the Risen One, Jesus Christ. Amen.

✻ ✻ ✻

Steadfast love and faithfulness will meet;
    righteousness and peace will kiss each other.
Faithfulness will spring up from the ground,
    and righteousness will look down from the sky.
The LORD will give what is good,
    and our land will yield its increase.
Righteousness will go before him,
    and will make a path for his steps.

—Psalm 85:10–13

MONDAY

May all the nations praise you, O God, Lord of history; may all the peoples praise you. I give myself to you in praise, asking that you would make me an instrument of your glory in the earth this day. Lord Jesus, may your kingdom come. Amen.

Preserve my life, for I am devoted to you;
    save your servant who trusts in you.
You are my God; be gracious to me, O Lord,
    for to you do I cry all day long.

—Psalm 86:2–3

TUESDAY

God of all comfort, love-filled Trinity, I rest in you and worship your holy name. Thank you for lifting and sustaining me as I walk with you. Spirit of life, flow through my life today, I pray. Amen.

Gladden the soul of your servant,
    for to you, O Lord, I lift up my soul.
For you, O Lord, are good and forgiving,
    abounding in steadfast love to all who call on you.

—Psalm 86:4–5

WEDNESDAY

Lord God, help me to understand today that I walk in your presence; that your Spirit is all around; that your angels, saints, and martyrs are not far off; and that the most important realities in my life are mostly unseen. Holy Spirit, keep me alive to you today. May I have the mind of Christ and radiate your love, I pray, for your glory and the blessing of all around. Amen.

> Give ear, O LORD, to my prayer;
>   listen to my cry of supplication.
> In the day of my trouble I call on you,
>   for you will answer me.
>
> —Psalm 86:6–7

THURSDAY

Holy Lord, I marvel at the deep, self-giving love that bonds Father, Son, and Spirit together in Holy Trinity. I worship you and ask that I may show your love to you and to others today, in the Spirit of Jesus. Amen.

> All the nations you have made shall come
>   and bow down before you, O Lord,
>   and shall glorify your name.
> For you are great and do wondrous things;
>   you alone are God.
>
> —Psalm 86:9–10

FRIDAY

Lord God of beauty, thank you for all the lovely things you have made, showing and showering your grace, harmony, and power. I marvel at the intricacy of your creative work. May all your works praise you today, O Lord, and may I see your beauty in your world and in your saving plan, I pray through Jesus Christ. Amen.

> Teach me your way, O LORD,
> that I may walk in your truth;
> give me an undivided heart to revere your name.
> —Psalm 86:11

SATURDAY

Loving Lord, who set the stars in place, I bow before your majesty and marvel at your grace. Help me to live today in the certainty that you are all-powerful, and that your power is seen especially in your self-giving, self-restraint, and lovingkindness. Amen.

> I give thanks to you, O Lord my God, with my whole heart,
> and I will glorify your name forever.
> For great is your steadfast love toward me;
> you have delivered my soul from the depths of Sheol.
> —Psalm 86:12–13

WEEK TWELVE

SUNDAY

Lord Jesus, you showed through your life on earth the meaning of faith working through love. Fill me today with your loving Spirit, and work your love through me as I trust in you, I pray. Amen.

But you, O Lord, are a God merciful and gracious,
   slow to anger and abounding in steadfast love and faithfulness.
                                                                    —Psalm 86:15

MONDAY

Thank you, Lord, for your love for all people, and especially your compassion for the poor. Help me this day to share your love. May your Spirit be upon me, that I may proclaim and be good news to the poor and oppressed this and every day. Amen.

✻ ✻ ✻

Happy are those who consider the poor;
    the LORD delivers them in the day of trouble.
The LORD protects them and keeps them alive;
    they are called happy in the land.
You do not give them up to the will of their enemies.

—Psalm 41:1–2

TUESDAY

Spirit of God, Sovereign Lord, glory, honor, and praise be to you this day. I worship you, Holy Lord, with all my being. Guide and use me in your service today, I pray. Amen.

✻ ✻ ✻

O LORD, God of my salvation,
    when, at night, I cry out in your presence,
let my prayer come before you;
    incline your ear to my cry.

—Psalm 88:1–2

WEDNESDAY

Lord God, Holy Trinity, I worship and honor you, bowing in your presence at the beginning of this day. Open my eyes to signs of your truth, wisdom, and reconciling work as I walk before you, I pray, and may all I do and am reflect your glory. Amen.

✴ ✴ ✴

But I, O LORD, cry out to you;
   in the morning my prayer comes before you.
                    —Psalm 88:13

THURSDAY

I cast all my cares upon you this day, loving Lord. I worship you and ask that by your Spirit you would help me to see all my life in light of your purposes and promises, and to rest in your grace. Amen.

✴ ✴ ✴

I will sing of your steadfast love, O LORD, forever;
   with my mouth I will proclaim your faithfulness to all generations.
I declare that your steadfast love is established forever;
   your faithfulness is as firm as the heavens.

                    —Psalm 89:1–2

FRIDAY

O God, Blessed Trinity, I praise you that you have created us for community. Thank you for the fellowship of sisters and brothers in Christ. Lord Jesus, help me this day to be a servant of your body, I pray. Amen.

✻ ✻ ✻

And let us consider how to provoke one another to love and good deeds, not neglecting to meet together, as is the habit of some, but encouraging one another, and all the more as you see the Day approaching.

—Hebrews 10:24–25

SATURDAY

Sovereign God, Holy Trinity, I worship you for your power and wisdom, but most of all for your shared and overflowing love. May I be joined in that love today and be a channel of your love to others, I pray. Amen.

✻ ✻ ✻

Before the mountains were brought forth,
    or ever you had formed the earth and the world,
    from everlasting to everlasting you are God.

—Psalm 90:2

WEEK THIRTEEN

SUNDAY

Loving, healing Father, I bow before you humbly, acknowledging my great need of you. When I fail to follow you fully and faithfully, forgive and touch me anew by your grace. Fill me freshly with your Spirit, that I may walk faithfully with you this day, I pray. Amen.

❋ ❋ ❋

Happy are those whose transgression is forgiven,
    whose sin is covered.
Happy are those to whom the LORD imputes no iniquity,
    and in whose spirit there is no deceit.

—Psalm 32:1–2

MONDAY

Thank you, Lord, for the gentle rain of your Spirit. You hold times and seasons in your hand, and you refresh the face of the earth. Help me to walk in your truth and joy, renewed by your Spirit this day, I pray. Amen.

❋ ❋ ❋

> The heavens are yours, the earth also is yours;
> the world and all that is in it—you have founded them.
> —Psalm 89:11

TUESDAY

Holy, loving God, thank you for the gift and promise of a new day to serve you. I worship you for your care, and for going ahead of me this day. Help me now to follow faithfully in the footsteps of Jesus, I pray. Amen.

❋ ❋ ❋

> So teach us to number our days,
> that we may apply our hearts unto wisdom.
> —Psalm 90:12 KJV

WEDNESDAY

O God, let the beauty of Jesus be seen in me! Holy Spirit, grow in my life the passion and purity of Jesus Christ. Bring forth more and more of the character of Jesus, the integrity of truth, and the fruit of the Spirit, I pray. Amen.

✻ ✻ ✻

Satisfy us in the morning with your steadfast love,
so that we may rejoice and be glad all our days.
—Psalm 90:14

THURSDAY

Holy, Sovereign Lord, Maker of heaven and earth, I thank you that you watch as a mother over all your creation, and that you care especially for all your children. Thank you for your love for me. Help me be a channel of your compassion to the poor and lost and lonely this day, I pray. Amen.

✻ ✻ ✻

Let the favor of the Lord our God be upon us,
and prosper for us the work of our hands—
O prosper the work of our hands!
—Psalm 90:17

FRIDAY

Show me your way, O Lord, that I may walk with you. Thank you for your written Word, and for the Word made flesh in Christ Jesus. Lamb of God, help me walk in your ways today and bring glory to you, I pray. Amen.

✸ ✸ ✸

[Moses said to the LORD,] "Now if I have found favor in your sight, show me your ways, so that I may know you and find favor in your sight."

—Exodus 33:13

SATURDAY

O Lord, God of love, I praise your holy name. As I bow before you in worship, energize me by your Spirit for this day. May your love flow through me, that I may bring praise to you in all inward thoughts and outward acts, I pray. Amen.

✸ ✸ ✸

Those who love me, I will deliver;
    I will protect those who know my name.
When they call to me, I will answer them;
    I will be with them in trouble,
    I will rescue them and honor them.
With long life I will satisfy them,
    and show them my salvation.

—Psalm 91:14–16

WEEK FOURTEEN

SUNDAY

Lord Jesus, source of eternal salvation, I worship you and praise you for opening the way to life for all. I trust in you today. Help me live now to the praise of your glory, I pray. Amen.

It is good to give thanks to the LORD,
    to sing praises to your name, O Most High;
to declare your steadfast love in the morning,
    and your faithfulness by night,
to the music of the lute and the harp,
    to the melody of the lyre.

—Psalm 92:1–3

MONDAY

Holy, Sovereign, all-seeing God, I bow in humble awe before you at the beginning of this day. I worship and praise you and give myself anew to your purposes. Lord Jesus, be glorified in my life today, I pray. Amen.

✳ ✳ ✳

You, O LORD, have made me glad by your work;
at the works of your hands I sing for joy.

How great are your works, O LORD!
Your thoughts are very deep!
—Psalm 92:4–5

TUESDAY

Glory be to you, Lord Most High! I worship in wonder, awe, and praise at the beginning of this day. Light my path with your glory, I pray, that I may live to your praise. Amen.

✳ ✳ ✳

The LORD will not forsake his people;
he will not abandon his heritage;
for justice will return to the righteous,
and all the upright in heart will follow it.
—Psalm 94:14–15

WEDNESDAY

Holy Lord, full of compassion and grace, I pause at the beginning of this day to worship you and to re-center my life in you. Help me to live in your love and share your compassion with all I meet, I pray. Amen.

If the LORD had not been my help,
    my soul would soon have lived in the land of silence.
When I thought, "My foot is slipping,"
    your steadfast love, O LORD, held me up.

—Psalm 94:17–18

THURSDAY

Jesus, Lord of history and Lord of my life, I bow before you now in joyful worship. I praise you for your redeeming love, and for your presence with me day by day. Keep me in your grace this day, I pray. Amen.

When the cares of my heart are many,
    your consolations cheer my soul.

—Psalm 94:19

FRIDAY

Thank you, O Lord, for your promise that your love endures forever. I rest in your love and ask for the ongoing transformation of my life by your love. Holy Spirit, let your love flow freely through my life today, I pray. Amen.

✺ ✺ ✺

But the LORD has become my stronghold,
and my God the rock of my refuge.
—Psalm 94:22

SATURDAY

Lord Jesus, thank you for your guidance and strength and patient care. I worship you and renew my total commitment to you. Wash and empower me by your Spirit that my life may reflect your glory, I pray. Amen.

✺ ✺ ✺

For the LORD is a great God,
and a great King above all gods.
In his hand are the depths of the earth;
the heights of the mountains are his also.
The sea is his, for he made it,
and the dry land, which his hands have formed.
—Psalm 95:3–5

WEEK FIFTEEN

SUNDAY

O God, you promise that your Spirit will fill the temple, and in time the whole earth fully. Dwell in me today, and renew your church, I pray. Speed the time when the earth shall be full of your knowledge, and help me play my faithful, fruitful part. Amen.

✳ ✳ ✳

O come, let us sing to the LORD;
    let us make a joyful noise to the rock of our salvation!
Let us come into his presence with thanksgiving;
    let us make a joyful noise to him with songs of praise!
                         —Psalm 95:1–2

MONDAY

Lord Jesus, I come to you for help and comfort just now. I sense my profound need of you. Wash me anew in your grace. Live in me by your Spirit, that I may have strength to serve you with faith and joy, I pray. Amen.

❊ ❊ ❊

It feels so insignificant, and yet this is the liberating secret: I am precisely the gift God wants—in full and humble surrender. . . . Saints are not uniform but are each unique creations of grace according to the journey God has led them through.

—Richard Rohr with Mike Morrell
The Divine Dance: The Trinity and Your Transformation

TUESDAY

Lord God of truth, Holy Trinity, I praise you today. O Lord, please form your people by your Word! Plant in our hearts the thirst and commitment to read your Word daily and feed on it by your Spirit so that we walk in the ways of Jesus, not the ways of the world with its violence, idolatries, and deceptions. Renew your church by Word and Spirit, I pray. Amen.

❊ ❊ ❊

It is not enough to have Bibles, but we must *use* them, yea, use them daily. Our souls must have constant meals of that manna which, if well digested, will afford them true nourishment and strength.

—John Wesley, commentary on Deuteronomy 17:19
Explanatory Notes upon the Old Testament

WEDNESDAY

God of wisdom, Spirit of truth, I bow now in worship before you, praising you and asking for your wisdom today. Give me discernment by your Spirit, that I may walk in your ways and reflect your truth, I pray. Amen.

✳ ✳ ✳

> Light dawns for the righteous,
>   and joy for the upright in heart.
> Rejoice in the LORD, O you righteous,
>   and give thanks to his holy name!
>   —Psalm 97:11–12

THURSDAY

Holy, loving Lord, thank you for your fresh grace this day. Thank you that your mercies are new every morning, and that you know and guide the way I take. May I gratefully be a channel of your grace to others, I pray. Amen.

✳ ✳ ✳

> O sing to the LORD a new song,
>   for he has done marvelous things.
> His right hand and his holy arm
>   have gotten him victory.
> The LORD has made known his victory;
>   he has revealed his vindication in the sight of the nations.
> He has remembered his steadfast love and faithfulness
>   to the house of Israel.
> All the ends of the earth have seen
>   the victory of our God.
>
>   —Psalm 98:1–3

FRIDAY

Holy, loving, caring Lord, you are my stronghold and my sure defense. I rest in you and worship you. Strengthen and help me to serve you so that today your will may be done on earth as it is in heaven. Amen.

Make a joyful noise to the LORD, all the earth;
  break forth into joyous song and sing praises.
Sing praises to the LORD with the lyre,
  with the lyre and the sound of melody.
With trumpets and the sound of the horn
  make a joyful noise before the King, the LORD.
—Psalm 98:4–6

SATURDAY

O Jesus, how wonderful you are; how wondrous your ways! How I praise and worship you! Pour out your love and power in my life today, I pray. May I come to this night in peace, knowing that I have walked with you and faithfully served your purposes. Amen.

Let the sea roar, and all that fills it;
  the world and those who live in it.
Let the floods clap their hands;
  let the hills sing together for joy
at the presence of the LORD, for he is coming
  to judge the earth.
He will judge the world with righteousness,
  and the peoples with equity.

—Psalm 98:7–9

WEEK SIXTEEN

SUNDAY

Holy, Holy, Holy Lord, Triune God of truth and love, I worship you now and confess you as God. I praise you for your love, freely given in Jesus Christ and working powerfully by your Spirit. Be glorified in my life today, I pray, as I seek to live to your praise. Amen.

✹ ✹ ✹

Holy is he!
Mighty King, lover of justice,
  you have established equity;
you have executed justice
  and righteousness in Jacob.
Extol the LORD our God;
  worship at his footstool.
  Holy is he!

—Psalm 99:3–5

MONDAY

Lord God, Maker of heaven and earth, I bow in worship today and lay my life, dreams, and hopes before you. I give my life to you for this day and forever, blessed Father, Son, and Holy Spirit. Amen.

※ ※ ※

Exalt the LORD our God,
  and worship at his holy hill;
  for the LORD our God is holy.
—Psalm 99:9 KJV

TUESDAY

Faithful, loving God, I thank you for the abundance of gifts and blessings you pour into our lives. Praise be to you, Holy Trinity. Make me a good and humble steward in your service, I pray, to the honor of Jesus Christ my Lord. Amen.

※ ※ ※

You make springs gush forth in the valleys;
  they flow between the hills,
giving drink to every wild animal;
  the wild asses quench their thirst.
By the streams the birds of the air have their habitation;
  they sing among the branches.
From your lofty abode you water the mountains;
  the earth is satisfied with the fruit of your work.
—Psalm 104:10–13

WEDNESDAY

Loving Savior, Lord of all creation, I bow in worship and awe before you at the beginning of this new day. Thank you for the gift of life and the promise of your presence. Holy Spirit, form the image of Christ more fully in me, I pray. Amen.

✳ ✳ ✳

O LORD, how manifold are your works!
In wisdom you have made them all;
the earth is full of your creatures.
—Psalm 104:24

THURSDAY

Holy, Holy, Holy Lord, God of power and might, I worship you in awe and wonder as this new day begins. Lord God, full of compassion, I praise you for revealing yourself to me and to your world. Help me to honor you in all I do and say, I pray. Amen.

✳ ✳ ✳

May the glory of the LORD endure forever;
may the LORD rejoice in his works—
who looks on the earth and it trembles,
who touches the mountains and they smoke.
—Psalm 104:31–32

FRIDAY

Jesus, Savior, Lord of history, I worship and honor you as I begin this day. Thank you, Dear Lord, for giving me life and leading me through the years. I renew my covenant with you for this new day. Guide me in right paths, I pray, that I may fulfill your purposes. Amen.

> I will not violate my covenant,
> or alter the word that went forth from my lips.
> —Psalm 89:34

SATURDAY

O Lord—God of truth, love, and determined purpose—I worship you now. Lord Jesus, please give me today confidence without arrogance, humility without self-abasement, courage without presumption, faith without fatalism, hope without sentimentality, and love without self-seeking, that I may follow you truly. Amen.

Truth is too high a price to pay for consistency. If you are deceived a dozen times a day, have the frankness and humility to confess it. It is a thousand times better to be true and honest than to be consistent in error. So long as you are too proud to admit mistakes, the Lord cannot lead you.

> —B. T. Roberts
> "Mistaken," *The Earnest Christian*

WEEK SEVENTEEN

SUNDAY

Holy, loving Lord, God of all creation, I worship you as I meditate in wonder on all your works. Blessed Trinity, open my heart more fully to you and to your world today, I pray. Amen.

> O give thanks to the LORD, call on his name,
>   make known his deeds among the peoples.
> Sing to him, sing praises to him;
>   tell of all his wonderful works.
> Glory in his holy name;
>   let the hearts of those who seek the LORD rejoice.
>   —Psalm 105:1–3

MONDAY

Dear Lord, God of all compassion, I worship you and wonder at your love, your grace, and the world you have made. Fill me with your loving Spirit today, I pray, and help me share your grace with others and live faithfully in your world. Amen.

> Why are you cast down, O my soul,
>   and why are you disquieted within me?
> Hope in God; for I shall again praise him,
>   my help and my God.
>
> —Psalm 42:11

TUESDAY

Blessed Savior, before whom all knees one day will bow, I worship you at the beginning of this day. I bow willingly before you and pray that you will help me walk in your ways, empowered by your Spirit. Amen.

> I will sing unto the LORD as long as I live: I will sing praise to my God
>   while I have my being.
> My meditation of him shall be sweet: I will be glad in the LORD.
>
> —Psalm 104:33–34 KJV

WEDNESDAY

O God of creation, redemption, and healing restoration, I bow before you in gratitude for your boundless grace, your lovingkindness. Lord Jesus, walk with me today in the power of the Spirit and to the glory of the Father, I pray. Amen.

Seek the LORD and his strength;
    seek his presence continually.
Remember the wonderful works he has done,
    his miracles, and the judgments he has uttered,
O offspring of his servant Abraham,
    children of Jacob, his chosen ones.

—Psalm 105:4–6

THURSDAY

O Lord, loving Spirit, help me be resolute, disciplined, determined, and undeterred in my devotion and my Christian walk today. Strengthen my will to do your will as I trust fully in the power of Jesus in my life, I pray. Amen.

Praise the LORD!
    O give thanks to the LORD, for he is good;
    for his steadfast love endures forever.

—Psalm 106:1

FRIDAY

O God, Lord of life and light, I worship you and lay my life before you at the beginning of this new day. Light my path and enliven my walk with you through every moment, I pray. May my life this day bring glory to you. Amen.

✳ ✳ ✳

Blessed be the God and Father of our Lord Jesus Christ, who has blessed us in Christ with every spiritual blessing in the heavenly places . . . He destined us for adoption as his children through Jesus Christ, according to the good pleasure of his will, to the praise of his glorious grace that he freely bestowed on us in the Beloved.

—Ephesians 1:3, 5–6

SATURDAY

Lord God, I would be true to you, regardless of the pressures, temptations, or distractions that would draw me from you. Holy Spirit, work quietly in my life today that inwardly and outwardly I may honor Jesus in all I think, do, and say. Amen.

✳ ✳ ✳

Who can utter the mighty doings of the LORD,
     or declare all his praise?
Happy are those who observe justice,
     who do righteousness at all times.

—Psalm 106:2–3

WEEK EIGHTEEN

SUNDAY

Holy, Holy, loving Lord, God of all creation, I worship you as I meditate in wonder on all your works. Blessed Trinity, open my heart more fully to you and to your world today, I pray. Amen.

I will give thanks to you, O LORD, among the peoples,
    and I will sing praises to you among the nations.
For your steadfast love is higher than the heavens,
    and your faithfulness reaches to the clouds.

—Psalm 108:3–4

MONDAY

Almighty God, since your Holy Word begins with the injunction to care for the garden (see Genesis 2:15) and ends with the warning that the time is coming "for destroying those who destroy the earth" (Rev. 11:18), help me to be a caring steward of your good creation, upon whose flourishing all life and every family of earth depend. I pray in Jesus' name. Amen.

❊ ❊ ❊

> Be exalted, O God, above the heavens,
> and let your glory be over all the earth.
> —Psalm 108:5

TUESDAY

Lord Jesus, King of the universe, I worship you and bow gladly in your presence this day. How great you are; how wonderful your purposes! Precious Jesus, be with me today and help me to walk in your ways, I pray. Amen.

❊ ❊ ❊

> Great are the works of the LORD,
> studied by all who delight in them.
> Full of honor and majesty is his work,
> and his righteousness endures forever.
> He has gained renown by his wonderful deeds;
> the LORD is gracious and merciful.
> —Psalm 111:2–4

WEDNESDAY

O Lord, here I am with you at this passing moment in time and space. Yet when I pray it seems space and time fade away, and I am with you timelessly, in eternity, all reality in view. I trust in you, who know the end from the beginning. Guide me today in my life here and now, I pray. Amen.

✦ ✦ ✦

When seeking God's guidance, trust your high moments.
—Alice Hayes Taylor (Mrs. J. Hudson Taylor II)

THURSDAY

Holy Lord, Blessed Trinity, I bow in awe and wonder before you at the opening of this day. I acknowledge you as beyond all time, and yet fully engaged in time and history. Help me this day to walk in your time and fulfill my part in your story, I pray. Amen.

✦ ✦ ✦

The fear of the LORD is the beginning of wisdom: a good understanding have all they that do his commandments: his praise [endures] for ever.
—Psalm 111:10 KJV

FRIDAY

O Lord, as you promised Moses, "My presence will go with you, and I will give you rest," so I ask for your presence to guide me today. Be with me and lead me to your perfect rest, I pray. Amen.

[Moses said to the LORD,] "Now if have found favor in your sight, show me your ways, so that I may know you and find favor in your sight. Consider too that this nation is your people." [The LORD] said, "My presence will go with you, and I will give you rest."

—Exodus 33:13–14

SATURDAY

Lord Jesus, Bright Morning Star, I worship you at the dawn of this new day. Thank you for your promise that you go before us, lighting the way, and that you will lead me and all your people to the new heaven and new earth. Amen.

And the Word became flesh and lived among us, and we have seen his glory, the glory as of a father's only son, full of grace and truth. . . . From his fullness we have all received, grace upon grace.

—John 1:14, 16

WEEK NINETEEN

SUNDAY

O God, as Moses' face reflected your glory, so may your glory shine through my life today. I pause now in your presence to seek your face. Fill me with your Spirit of grace and love for this day, I pray. Amen.

Praise the LORD!
I will give thanks to the LORD with my whole heart,
in the company of the upright, in the congregation.
—Psalm 111:1

MONDAY

Jesus, Savior, hope of the world and all creation, I bow joyfully before you today, praising your holy name. Thank you, Lord Jesus, for your wonderful path of salvation, the Way. Blessed Jesus, live in me today that others may share in your grace, I pray. Amen.

Praise the LORD!
Happy are those who fear the LORD,
who greatly delight in his commandments.
—Psalm 112:1

TUESDAY

Blessed, loving Savior, I open my mind and heart fully to you today. O God, search me and try me; cleanse me from all that fights your good purposes. Be deeply in my mind, heart, and imagination, I pray, for your glory. Amen.

Blessed be the name of the LORD
from this time on and forevermore.
From the rising of the sun to its setting
the name of the LORD is to be praised.
The LORD is high above all nations,
and his glory above the heavens.
—Psalm 113:2–4

WEDNESDAY

Sovereign Lord, Master of history, I thank you that you are working out your purposes in your way, and that by your grace I can play a small but essential part. I honor you today. Help me to live fully in your will in all I do, think, or say, I pray. Amen.

Tremble, O earth, at the presence of the LORD,
  at the presence of the God of Jacob,
who turns the rock into a pool of water,
  the flint into a spring of water.

—Psalm 114:7–8

THURSDAY

O Jesus, delight of my soul, I bow before you today in joy and praise, thanking you for your mercy and presence and guidance from day to day. Lead me now and always, until the day I see you face-to-face, I pray. Amen.

[Jesus] shall reign over the house of Jacob for ever; and of his kingdom there shall be no end.

—Luke 1:33 KJV

FRIDAY

Holy, loving Lord, praise be to you, now and evermore! I open my mind and heart to you. I breathe out all my self-preoccupation and breathe in your cleansing, focusing Holy Spirit. Help me to walk in peace and close fellowship with you today, I pray. Amen.

> I love the LORD, because he has heard
>   my voice and my supplications.
> Because he inclined his ear to me,
>   therefore I will call on him as long as I live.
> —Psalm 116:1–2

SATURDAY

O God, pure love, my prayer rises to you at the dawn of this new day. How great you are, full of kindness and compassion. O Lord, work in my life by your Holy Spirit, that I may be like Jesus. I pray in Jesus' name. Amen.

> Gracious is the LORD, and righteous;
>   our God is merciful.
> The LORD protects the simple;
>   when I was brought low, he saved me.
> Return, O my soul, to your rest,
>   for the LORD has dealt bountifully with you.
> —Psalm 116:5–7

WEEK TWENTY

SUNDAY

Lord God, I thank you that you are rich in mercy and compassion. Thank you for your transforming grace in my life. Help me this day to embody the mercy you showed in Jesus Christ, through the power of the Holy Spirit, I pray. Amen.

But God, who is rich in mercy, out of the great love with which he loved us even when we were dead through our trespasses, made us alive together with Christ. . . .

—Ephesians 2:4–5

Monday

Praise, honor, and glory be to you, God Most High. I come to you today in need and in hope. I trust in you and thank you that you will supply my need of grace. Holy, loving Lord, be in my mind and heart and actions this day, I pray, to the glory of your name. Amen.

> O give thanks to the LORD, for he is good;
>   his steadfast love endures forever! . . .
> Let those who fear the LORD say,
>   "His steadfast love endures forever."
>   —Psalm 118:1, 4

Tuesday

O God, whose depth of mercy is beyond comprehension, I worship you and humbly accept your love and guidance today. Work so deeply in my heart by your Spirit that your mercy shown in Jesus may flow through me to others, I pray, to the glory of your name. Amen.

No one will ever go into despair while he feels God cares for him.
                                 —B. T. Roberts
            Sermon on Ephesians 2:4–7, *The Earnest Christian*

WEDNESDAY

Lord Jesus, I need you today. My hope and strength and joy are in you. In weakness I bow before you. I praise and worship you, asking that your Spirit would give me grace and wisdom to walk with you in all I do. Praise and honor be to you, loving Lord. Amen.

✳ ✳ ✳

The sacrifice acceptable to God is a broken spirit;
a broken and contrite heart, O God, you will not despise.
—Psalm 51:17

THURSDAY

For all your good gifts to me, O Lord, I give you praise. Thank you for your lovingkindness and your constant mercy. May I walk faithfully in your grace this day, I pray, lifted and led by your Holy Spirit. Amen.

✳ ✳ ✳

Happy are those whose way is blameless,
who walk in the law of the LORD.
Happy are those who keep his decrees,
who seek him with their whole heart,
who also do no wrong,
but walk in his ways.
—Psalm 119:1–3

FRIDAY

Lord Jesus, who gave your life for me and for the life of the world, I bow in worship and praise before you once again. May my gratitude to you well up in praise and faithful service all through this day, I pray. Amen.

> With my whole heart I seek you;
>   do not let me stray from your commandments.
> I treasure your word in my heart,
>   so that I may not sin against you.
> Blessed are you, O LORD;
>   teach me your statutes.
>
> —Psalm 119:10–12

SATURDAY

O God, your Word reminds us in many ways that the battle is the Lord's. I acknowledge your power and wisdom and give myself to you to do your work in your way. Lord Jesus, live in my life by your Spirit today, that your purposes may succeed through me. Amen.

> I delight in the way of your decrees
>   as much as in all riches.
> I will meditate on your precepts,
>   and fix my eyes on your ways.
> I will delight in your statutes;
>   I will not forget your word.
>
> —Psalm 119:14–16

WEEK TWENTY-ONE

SUNDAY

Lord God of righteousness and justice, I thank you that you have made a moral universe, and that you work justice in the land. O God, may your kingdom come, putting down oppression and injustice, and bringing your perfect healing and peace, I pray. Amen.

* * *

The LORD works vindication
and justice for all who are oppressed.
—Psalm 103:6

MONDAY

Thank you, Lord, for the good earth and all the varied and clever creatures you have made. Help me live to your glory today, and to do my part in caring for your world, until you bring new heavens and new earth, I pray. Amen.

✳ ✳ ✳

Open my eyes, so that I may behold
wondrous things out of your law.
I live as an alien in the land;
do not hide your commandments from me.
—Psalm 119:18–19

TUESDAY

Lord God, I thank you for your motherly care of all you have made. I praise you for your love and tender mercies, and for the power of your love to transform and heal. Help me to nurture others, that they may see you in me, I pray. Amen.

✳ ✳ ✳

The LORD is merciful and gracious, slow to anger,
and plenteous in mercy.
—Psalm 103:8 KJV

WEDNESDAY

Lord God of all truth and knowledge, I worship you and seek your wisdom today. In this age of Internet and social media, guide me in your truth. Lead me by your Spirit; fill me with Jesus' love. Help me speak or keep silence as will most glorify you and fulfill your good purposes, I pray. Amen.

✳ ✳ ✳

"Let your word be 'Yes, Yes' or 'No, No'; anything more than this comes from the evil one."

—Jesus (Matthew 5:37)

THURSDAY

Lord God, I pray to you today because I have confidence that you hear, deeply understand, and act in my life and throughout your whole creation. Lord Jesus, form your own character within me through your strong, loving Spirit, I pray. Amen.

✳ ✳ ✳

Your decrees are my delight,
they are my counselors.
—Psalm 119:24

FRIDAY

O Lord, you have said, "In quietness and confidence will be your strength." I give myself anew to you. Help me to live quietly in your presence today, with full confidence in you and your good purposes and sure promises. Amen.

✳ ✳ ✳

Thus says the LORD GOD, the Holy One of Israel; In returning and rest you shall be saved; in quietness and in confidence shall be your strength. . . .

—Isaiah 30:15 KJV (author's paraphrase)

SATURDAY

O Lord, you require truth in the inward life and in outward living. I bow before you in worship, asking that you will cleanse and fill me today, that I may honor you and walk in your truth. May every thought, word, deed, be love. Amen.

✳ ✳ ✳

> Put false ways far from me;
>   and graciously teach me your law.
> I have chosen the way of faithfulness;
>   I set your ordinances before me.
>   —Psalm 119:29–30

WEEK TWENTY-TWO

SUNDAY

O God, Blessed Trinity, I want to honor you in all I do and say. I focus my mind and heart on you, asking for a fresh touch of your Holy Spirit. Dear Jesus, walk with me and help me walk with you throughout this day, I pray. Amen.

> I cling to your decrees, O LORD;
>   let me not be put to shame.
> I run the way of your commandments,
>   for you enlarge my understanding.
>   —Psalm 119:31–32

MONDAY

I thank you, O God, that your grace is sufficient—for me, for all who come to you in true faith, for your whole creation. Thank you, Blessed Trinity, for abounding grace and goodness. Help me to receive and show forth your grace this day, I pray through Jesus Christ, by your Spirit, to the glory of the Father. Amen.

✳ ✳ ✳

As a father has compassion for his children,
    so the LORD has compassion for those who fear him.
For he knows how we were made;
    he remembers that we are dust.

—Psalm 103:13–14

TUESDAY

O God, you say in your Word: maintain justice for the poor! Lord, may your Word be heard and heeded throughout the earth, and in the church and my life. Holy Spirit, give me the wisdom and courage to serve the poor today, through Jesus Christ my Lord. Amen.

✳ ✳ ✳

All your works shall give thanks to you, O LORD,
    and all your faithful shall bless you.
They shall speak of the glory of your kingdom,
    and tell of your power,
to make known to all people your mighty deeds,
    and the glorious splendor of your kingdom.

—Psalm 145:10–12

WEDNESDAY

O God, who long ago sent the plagues on Egypt and hardened Pharaoh's heart, I acknowledge your sovereign power over nature and history and nations. Thank you for acting in Jesus Christ to bring salvation, and for continually sending your Holy Spirit to soften hearts and draw people and nations to yourself. Amen.

Turn my heart to your decrees,
and not to selfish gain.
Turn my eyes from looking at vanities;
give me life in your ways.
Confirm to your servant your promise,
which is for those who fear you.
—Psalm 119:36–38

THURSDAY

Sovereign Lord, your Word speaks of "the wine of God's fury" being "poured full strength into the cup of his wrath." Repeatedly you speak judgment against all that defies and defiles your purposes. Help me this day to be a faithful agent of your mercy and truth, even as I trust fully in your promise to bring justice, judgment, and peace to your whole creation. Amen.

"If anyone worships the beast and its image and receives its mark on their forehead or on their hand, they, too, will drink the wine of God's fury, which has been poured full strength into the cup of his wrath."
—Revelation 14:9–10 NIV

FRIDAY

Lamb of God, who takes away the sin of the world, I worship you and give my mind, heart, and will to serve you today. Blessed Holy Spirit, work in my life that I may be a faithful witness to Jesus Christ, to the glory of the Father, I pray. Amen.

✳ ✳ ✳

I find my delight in your commandments,
because I love them.
I revere your commandments, which I love,
and I will meditate on your statutes.
—Psalm 119:47–48

SATURDAY

Lord God, Maker of earth and heaven, Creator of worlds, I praise and worship you. Thank you for your love that reaches as far as your power. Help me walk in the light of your grace today through Jesus Christ in the power of your Spirit. Amen.

✳ ✳ ✳

Make me understand the way of your precepts:
so shall I talk of your wondrous works.
—Psalm 119:27 KJV (author's paraphrase)

WEEK TWENTY-THREE

SUNDAY

Holy, loving, Triune God, I pause in quietness before you as I begin this day. Help me to see all things in the universe, and my own life, in the light of your truth, love, and justice, I pray. Go with and before me as I seek to worship and serve you. Amen.

Remember your word to your servant,
    in which you have made me hope.
This is my comfort in my distress,
    that your promise gives me life.
                        —Psalm 119:49–50

MONDAY

O God, Sovereign of the universe, I bow in humble worship at the beginning of this day. I acknowledge your supreme power and your tender love. Strengthen me and help me to honor you in all I do. May your love and truth shine through me, I pray. Amen.

✳ ✳ ✳

Your statutes have been my songs
  wherever I make my home.
I remember your name in the night, O LORD,
  and keep your law.
                                    —Psalm 119:54–55

TUESDAY

Jesus, Jesus, Jesus! Holy Lord and Savior! I need you today. I bow in worship, praising you and seeking your help as I begin a new day. Blessed Savior, live in me and keep me in your care, I pray. Amen.

✳ ✳ ✳

You have dealt well with your servant,
  O LORD, according to your word.
Teach me good judgment and knowledge,
  for I believe in your commandments.
                                    —Psalm 119:65–66

WEDNESDAY

Lord God of time, space, and creation, I worship you. From solstice to equinox, from equinox to solstice, you are Lord, Creator, Sustainer, Healer, Coherence-bringer. Help me walk season by season in your ways, following Jesus, led by your Spirit, I pray. Amen.

✳ ✳ ✳

The earth, O LORD, is full of thy mercy: teach me thy statutes.
—Psalm 119:64 KJV

THURSDAY

My heart is full of praise to you, O Lord, as I come before you at the dawn of this new day. Thank you for your love, your compassion, and your tender mercies. Through Jesus Christ, I ask that you would give me the grace to serve and honor you and to live to your praise. Amen.

✳ ✳ ✳

You are good and do good;
teach me your statutes.
—Psalm 119:68

FRIDAY

Faithful, loving God, I praise and worship you as I bow now in your presence. I am awed by your love, your fiery holiness, your sovereign power. Yet you say, "Come to me!" O Lord, I come, I come, and I lay my life before you and open my heart to you this day. Amen.

✷ ✷ ✷

[Your] hands have made me and fashioned me: give me understanding, that I may learn [your] commandments.

—Psalm 119:73 KJV

SATURDAY

Holy God, Blessed Trinity, I worship you at the start of another day. I am weak, but you are strong. Thank you for your strengthening, self-giving, inexplicable love. May I honor you in all I do this day, I pray. Amen.

✷ ✷ ✷

I know, O LORD, that your judgments are right,
and that in faithfulness you have humbled me.
Let your steadfast love become my comfort
according to your promise to your servant.
Let your mercy come to me, that I may live;
for your law is my delight.

—Psalm 119:75–77

WEEK TWENTY-FOUR

SUNDAY

Lord God, I confess today that you are God and that this is my Father's world. I rest in the reality of all you have made and the larger truth of your creative and redemptive purposes. Help me this day to honor you and to see you in your world and your acts, I pray. Amen.

※ ※ ※

It is the work of the Holy Spirit to make us *more* physical, *more* material, not less so—that is, to make us fully human. By the Spirit we become more like Jesus, the Word who was made flesh, not just spirit, and rose in the flesh, not solely spirit. True spirituality is true physicality—now and on into the new creation, when earth and heaven are one.

MONDAY

I join my heart and voice with all creation in praising you this day, blessed Father, Son, and Holy Spirit. You have built joy into all you have made, despite death and suffering. O God, fill me with the joy of your Spirit today, and help me walk in the way of Jesus, who bravely endured pain for the joy set before him. Amen.

❊ ❊ ❊

[Look] to Jesus the pioneer and perfecter of our faith, who for the sake of the joy that was set before him endured the cross, disregarding its shame, and has taken his seat at the right hand of the throne of God.

Consider him who endured such hostility against himself from sinners, so that you may not grow weary or lose heart.

—Hebrews 12:2–3

TUESDAY

O God, the deep desire of my heart today is to worship you and honor you and love you more fully. Blessed Holy Spirit, work deeply in my spirit today, that the beauty of Jesus may be seen in me. Amen.

❊ ❊ ❊

Spirit of God, descend upon my heart;
wean it from sin, through all its pulses
move;
stoop to my weakness, mighty as thou
art,
and help me love thee as I ought to love.
—George Croly, "Spirit of God,
Descend upon My Heart," 1867, rev.

Help me to love the earth which you
have made,
Help me to trust your world-renewing
power.
Revive your church, O grant us now
your aid,
Spirit of Christ, in this, earth's needy hour.
—H. A. Snyder, 2016

WEDNESDAY

Lord God, who showed your power to Pharaoh when you delivered Israel from Egypt, I acknowledge your sovereignty over peoples, nations, and the forces of nature. I bow in worship before you. Help me this day to know and honor you in all I do, to your glory and the serving of your purposes, I pray. Amen.

> May my heart be blameless in your statutes,
>   so that I may not be put to shame.
>   —Psalm 119:80

THURSDAY

Spirit of God, I worship you in your presence, in your essence, and open the doors and windows of my life to your influences today. Holy Spirit, breathe into all my life that I may be a fitting dwelling place for you and fully open to your work. Walk with me today as I seek to follow Jesus, I pray. Amen.

> In your steadfast love spare my life,
>   so that I may keep the decrees of your mouth.
>   —Psalm 119:88

FRIDAY

Blessed Trinity, I worship you, bowing in awe and joy before you. Holy Lord, be glorified in my life today. May I walk with and serve Jesus Christ through the power of the Spirit, to the glory of the Father. May this day in its living be an acceptable offering to you, I pray. Amen.

> The LORD exists forever;
> your word is firmly fixed in heaven.
> Your faithfulness endures to all generations;
> you have established the earth, and it stands fast.
> By your appointment they stand today,
> for all things are your servants.

—Psalm 119:89–91

SATURDAY

Lord God, "Faithful and True" (Rev. 19:11), I bow before you in praise and worship. Thank you, Lord Jesus, for the victory you won and the life you lived, and for the name known only to you. Live in me by your Spirit today, I pray, that my life may bring glory to you; that I may be faithful and true. Amen.

> Then I saw heaven opened, and there was a white horse! Its rider is called Faithful and True, and in righteousness he judges and makes war. His eyes are like a flame of fire, and on his head are many diadems; and he has a name inscribed that no one knows but himself.

—Revelation 19:11–12

WEEK TWENTY-FIVE

SUNDAY

Holy Lord, who knows the end from the beginning, I bow in your presence and open my heart and mind to you. You know all that I am and all I long to be. I give myself to you, that I may serve you and that you may accomplish your will in and through me today. Amen.

> I will never forget your precepts,
>   for by them you have given me life.
> I am yours; save me,
>   for I have sought your precepts.
>   —Psalm 119:93–94

MONDAY

O Lord, I hear your call to holiness. You say, "Be holy, for I am holy." Fill me Lord with your Spirit today, that your holiness may be seen in me, and that I may bring glory to you. Through Jesus Christ I pray. Amen.

✳ ✳ ✳

For I am the LORD your God; sanctify yourselves therefore, and be holy, for I am holy. . . . For I am the LORD who brought you up from the land of Egypt, to be your God; you shall be holy, for I am holy.

—Leviticus 11:44–45

TUESDAY

Holy, Holy, Holy, Lord God Almighty! Heaven and earth are full of your glory. Lord God, I join my voice and my heart in praise to you. Help me to live in you and rejoice in your grace today, I pray. Amen.

✳ ✳ ✳

O LORD, our Sovereign,
   how majestic is your name in all the earth!
   You have set your glory above the heavens.

—Psalm 8:1

WEDNESDAY

Lord God of Abraham, Isaac, and Jacob, I thank you that you have been working all down through time to accomplish your purposes. I worship and honor you and trust your timing. Help me walk confidently and obediently with you today, I pray. Amen.

✻ ✻ ✻

I hold back my feet from every evil way,
    in order to keep your word.
I do not turn away from your ordinances,
    for you have taught me.
—Psalm 119:101–2

THURSDAY

Lord Jesus, I am moved today as I think of the consistency, power, compassion, and deep devotion to God that your earthly life displayed. Spirit of Jesus, be in my life today. Empower me to live the life you modeled, I pray. Amen.

✻ ✻ ✻

"For I have set you an example, that you also should do as I have done to you."

—Jesus (John 13:15)

FRIDAY

Lord God, you have made us to inhabit time and eternity, spirit and matter. Help me to understand this sufficiently so that I give proper place to the physical and to the spiritual. Help me especially, Lord Jesus, to be more concerned and careful about my spiritual health than about my physical well-being, while maintaining a godly balance. I pray in the name of the One who promises life in its fullness, life in wholeness. Amen.

How sweet are your words to my taste,
   sweeter than honey to my mouth!
Through your precepts I get understanding;
   therefore I hate every false way.
              —Psalm 119:103–4

SATURDAY

Dear Lord, as I walk with you day by day, help me to see things more clearly, love you more dearly, and follow you more nearly. Amen.
      —Based on the prayer of St. Richard of Chichester, c. 1197–1253

Your word is a lamp to my feet
   and a light to my path.
I have sworn an oath and confirmed it,
   to observe your righteous ordinances.
              —Psalm 119:105–6

WEEK TWENTY-SIX

SUNDAY

Holy Spirit of God, Spirit of Jesus, Spirit of light and truth, I worship you and give my life to your guidance today. Lord God, may I be led by your Spirit in all I think, say, do, intend, or imagine this day, I pray. Amen.

✳ ✳ ✳

> Your decrees are my heritage forever;
>   they are the joy of my heart.
> I incline my heart to perform your statutes
>   forever, to the end.
>
> —Psalm 119:111–12

MONDAY

Jesus, Lord and Risen One, I worship you and rejoice in your resurrection from the dead. Thank you that you are life and hold the keys to life. Help me bear witness to your life today through the power of your Spirit, I pray. Amen.

"I am the resurrection and the life. Those who believe in me, even though they die, will live, and everyone who lives and believes in me will never die."

—Jesus (John 11:25–26)

TUESDAY

Lord Jesus, God of all comfort, I bow before you today with joy in you, your presence, and your encouraging strength. As I renew my covenant with you, may your Spirit cleanse, fortify, and comfort so that all I do and say this day brings glory to you. Help me walk in your way and sing your praises, morning, noon, and night. Amen.

You are my hiding place and my shield;
I hope in your word.

—Psalm 119:114

WEDNESDAY

Lord God of our mothers and fathers and of all faithful Christians who have gone before, I thank you for your faithfulness over generations. Thank you for adopting me into your family through Jesus Christ. Help me walk faithfully before you today, as did your faithful servants in the past, I pray. Amen.

> Uphold me according to your promise, that I may live,
>   and let me not be put to shame in my hope.
> Hold me up, that I may be safe
>   and have regard for your statutes continually.
>
> —Psalm 119:116–17

THURSDAY

I thank you, Sovereign Lord, that you are both ultimate and intimate. I worship you today in love and wonder. Precious Jesus, I trust your ultimate will and purposes, and I ask for your intimate presence with me today, through your Living Holy Spirit. Amen.

God is both ultimate and intimate. The ultimate and intimate dimensions of God's love for every person and community must be held together.

> —A. H. Mathias Zahniser
> *Symbol and Ceremony: Making Disciples Across Cultures*

FRIDAY

O Lord, God of the poor, the oppressed, and the empty-handed, I worship you today for your compassion and constant love. Thank you that you hear the cry of the needy. Lord Jesus, help me hear the cries of the poor today, and to engage in your work of setting captives free. Amen.

If you close your ear to the cry of the poor,
you will cry out and not be heard.
—Proverbs 21:13

SATURDAY

O God, who would fold both heaven and earth in a single peace: let the design of your great love light upon the waste of our wraths and sorrows, and give peace to your church, peace among nations, peace in our dwellings, and peace in our hearts, through your Son our Savior Jesus Christ.
—Adapted from *Daily Prayer*

Deal with your servant according to your steadfast love,
and teach me your statutes.
I am your servant; give me understanding,
so that I may know your decrees.
—Psalm 119:124–25

WEEK TWENTY-SEVEN

SUNDAY

Help me, Lord, in the work of prayer. Help me bear faithfully and hopefully the burden of intercession. Thank you, Lord Jesus, for bearing us up in prayer; that you live constantly interceding for us (Heb. 7:25); that your Holy Spirit intercedes "with sighs too deep for words," according to your will. O Lord, may your kingdom come, I pray. Amen.

✻ ✻ ✻

Likewise the Spirit helps us in our weakness; for we do not know how to pray as we ought, but that very Spirit intercedes with sighs too deep for words. And God, who searches the heart, knows what is the mind of the Spirit, because the Spirit intercedes for the saints according to the will of God. . . .

It is Christ Jesus, who died, yes, who was raised, who is at the right hand of God, who indeed intercedes for us.

—Romans 8:26–27, 34

MONDAY

Holy Lord, I would be holy today not according to human ideas but according to your Word and the character of Jesus. Form your righteousness and true loving holiness, the mind of Christ, in my life through your Holy Spirit, I pray. Amen.

✳ ✳ ✳

The character of Jesus is becoming the silent Judge of all things.

—E. Stanley Jones
Christ at the Round Table

TUESDAY

Lord Jesus, I praise you for the joy of knowing you through the ministry of the Spirit and of serving you this day. Holy Father, be glorified in all I think, say, and do from morning to night, I pray. Amen.

✳ ✳ ✳

Jesus rejoiced in the Holy Spirit and said, "I thank you, Father, Lord of heaven and earth, because you have hidden these things from the wise and the intelligent and have revealed them to infants; yes, Father, for such was your gracious will. All things have been handed over to me by my Father; and no one knows who the Son is except the Father, or who the Father is except the Son and anyone to whom the Son chooses to reveal him."

—Luke 10:21–22

WEDNESDAY

Holy Lord, God of the universe, I worship humbly before you in awe and wonder. I would be lost in wonder alone, had you not revealed yourself as love and compassion and inner transformation through Jesus Christ. Lord, by your Spirit continue to reveal yourself in my life today, I pray, for the sake of your world. Amen.

> Your decrees are wonderful;
>   therefore my soul keeps them.
> The unfolding of your words gives light;
>   it imparts understanding to the simple.
> —Psalm 119:129–30

THURSDAY

O Lord, I enter now that "place of quiet rest, near to the heart of God." Dear Jesus, I draw near to you that you may draw near to me. Open your heart to me as I worship you and rest in your presence, I pray. Amen.

> There is a place of quiet rest, near to the heart of God;
> A place where sin cannot molest, near to the heart of God.
> O Jesus, blest Redeemer, sent from the heart of God,
> Hold us, who wait before Thee, near to the heart of God.
> —Cleland B. McAfee,
> "Near to the Heart of God," 1903

FRIDAY

Loving, Holy God, I want Jesus to walk with me today. I worship you and I give my life and my way into your hands. As I journey through this day, may I walk by your side and be led by your Spirit, I pray. Amen.

✳ ✳ ✳

Keep my steps steady according to your promise,
and never let iniquity have dominion over me.
—Psalm 119:133

SATURDAY

O Lord, you have said that your people would "inherit the land." I worship you today and acknowledge your sovereign care over all creation—soil, snails, and stars. Help me be a good steward of the beautiful world you have made and live faithfully before you so that the whole earth may be full of your glory, until you create new heavens and earth, restoring and making all things new. Amen.

✳ ✳ ✳

But the meek shall inherit the earth;
and shall delight themselves in the abundance of peace. . . .
The righteous shall inherit the land,
and dwell therein for ever.

—Psalm 37:11, 29 KJV

WEEK TWENTY-EIGHT

SUNDAY

Jesus, you have said that those who hunger and thirst for righteousness would be filled. I hunger and thirst for more of you. Increase my appetite for you, my thirst for your truth, that your Spirit may work in and through me for your kingdom purposes and to your glory, I pray. Amen.

"Blessed are those who hunger and thirst for righteousness, for they will be filled.

"Blessed are the merciful, for they will receive mercy."

—Jesus (Matthew 5:6–7)

MONDAY

Jesus, Jesus, Blessed Savior! I worship you now with joy and deep gratitude for your presence and the life you give. Holy Savior, act in my life today and strengthen my will to do your will, I pray. May I live to your glory. Amen.

✸ ✸ ✸

Make your face shine upon your servant,
and teach me your statutes.

—Psalm 119:135

TUESDAY

Lord God of salvation, I thank you for the thousands who are coming to know you day by day throughout the world. Praise to you, Lord Jesus, for the great multitude from every people and land that you are now forming. Blessed Holy Spirit, work in me today for the health, integrity, and extension of your church, I pray. Amen.

✸ ✸ ✸

Your righteousness is an everlasting righteousness,
and your law is the truth.

—Psalm 119:142

WEDNESDAY

Thank you, Triune God, for Christian fellowship. Be with me today in all my relationships with sisters and brothers in the body of Christ. Holy Spirit, help us help each other grow in grace. Graciously may I both give and receive. Lord Jesus, may your healing power renew your body so that through your people the world will come to know you, I pray. Amen.

> With my whole heart I cry; answer me, O LORD.
>   I will keep your statutes.
> I cry to you; save me,
>   that I may observe your decrees.
> I rise before dawn and cry for help;
>   I put my hope in your words.
> My eyes are awake before each watch of the night,
>   that I may meditate on your promise.
>   —Psalm 119:145–48

THURSDAY

O God, you are sovereign over all things—all peoples and nations, all the earth, all the energies of nature. Yet you give us the freedom to follow you freely. Thank you for your convicting, persuading, nudging, and saving grace. Help me walk in your ways with joy and faithfulness today, fully open to your Spirit, I pray. Amen.

> In your steadfast love hear my voice;
>   O LORD, in your justice preserve my life.
>   —Psalm 119:149

FRIDAY

O God of love and wisdom, you understand better than I the complex interplay of body, mind, and will, of spirit and flesh. Live in *all* my life today by your Spirit, I pray. Throughout this day, in all I do, may every thought, word, deed, be love. Amen.

✻ ✻ ✻

[May] the very God of peace sanctify you wholly; and I pray God your whole spirit and soul and body be preserved blameless unto the coming of our Lord Jesus Christ.

—1 Thessalonians 5:23 KJV

SATURDAY

Lord Jesus, there is much I do not understand about you, your ways, and the working of your purposes in history and in my life. But I trust you. Blessed Savior, surround me with your loving presence this day, and help me to trust where I cannot see. Amen.

✻ ✻ ✻

Consider how I love your precepts;
    preserve my life according to your steadfast love.
The sum of your word is truth;
    and every one of your righteous ordinances endures forever.

—Psalm 119:159–60

WEEK TWENTY-NINE

SUNDAY

O God of power and lovingkindness and tender mercy, I rest in you today. "All my trust on Thee is stayed, all my help from Thee I bring." I pledge my life wholly to your service. Keep me in your paths, trusting in your grace this day, I pray. Amen.

✳ ✳ ✳

Other refuge have I none, hangs my helpless soul on Thee;
Leave, ah! leave me not alone, still support and comfort me.
All my trust on Thee is stayed, all my help from Thee I bring;
Cover my defenseless head with the shadow of Thy wing.
—Charles Wesley,
"Jesus, Lover of My Soul" 1740

MONDAY

O God, you have said it is your purpose to give your people "hope and a future." Thank you for your good and perfect promises. Fulfill your purposes in and for me, I pray. May your kingdom come and your will be done on earth as in heaven. Amen.

✳ ✳ ✳

"For I know the plans I have for you," declares the LORD, "plans to prosper you and not to harm you, plans to give you hope and a future."

—Jeremiah 29:11 NIV

TUESDAY

Lord of truth and divine purpose, help me lead a reflective life. In the rush of short-term, small-aim activity and distractions, help me to pause, to measure my ways, to order my life so as to reflect your time and purposes, I pray. Amen.

✳ ✳ ✳

I remember the days of old,
    I think about all your deeds,
    I meditate on the works of your hands.
I stretch out my hands to you;
    my soul thirsts for you like a parched land.

—Psalm 143:5–6

WEDNESDAY

Lord Jesus, I want this to be a day of utter faithfulness to you. I worship you and bow in your presence, asking for the fullness of your Spirit in all I do and say. Keep me in your grace and use me to your purposes, I pray. Amen.

> Hear my prayer, O LORD;
> > give ear to my supplications in your faithfulness;
> > answer me in your righteousness.

—Psalm 143:1

THURSDAY

Lord God, Holy Trinity, my heart is full of praise to you this day. I worship and exalt you for your love and mercy and power; for your ways, which are "past finding out" (Rom. 11:33 KJV). Lord Jesus, may I honor you throughout this day in every way, and rest in you this night, I pray. Amen.

> Let me hear of your steadfast love in the morning,
> > for in you I put my trust.
> Teach me the way I should go,
> > for to you I lift up my soul.

—Psalm 143:8

FRIDAY

Holy, Holy, Holy Lord, heaven and earth are full of your glory. Lord God, I join my voice with the millions of people around the world who worship you this day. May all the people praise you! May my life today be praise, I ask through Jesus Christ. Amen.

> Teach me to do your will,
> for you are my God.
> Let your good spirit lead me
> on a level path.
> —Psalm 143:10

SATURDAY

I sing praise to you at the beginning of this new day, Holy Lord. Praise be to you for your love, your mercy, and your guiding providence over time and history. Help me walk in your Spirit today in faithful service to Jesus, I pray. Amen.

> Great peace have those who love your law;
> nothing can make them stumble.
> I hope for your salvation, O LORD,
> and I fulfill your commandments.
> —Psalm 119:165–66

SUNDAY

O God, Lord of sea and sky, trees and vast mountain ranges, I honor you and your power, wisdom, and effulgence of beauty. Dear Father, make me more like you. Form the image of Jesus fully in all areas of my life today, through your Holy Spirit, I pray. Amen.

❊ ❊ ❊

All of us, with unveiled faces, seeing the glory of the Lord as though reflected in a mirror, are being transformed into the same image from one degree of glory to another; for this comes from the Lord, the Spirit.

—2 Corinthians 3:18

MONDAY

Thank you, Lord God, for showing the meaning of true life and genuine living in Jesus Christ. O Lord, I want to be like Jesus! Holy Spirit, work in me your good purposes today, that I may be holy as you are holy. Amen.

✳ ✳ ✳

For to this you have been called, because Christ also suffered for you, leaving you an example, so that you should follow in his steps.

—1 Peter 2:21

TUESDAY

Dear loving Mother God, source of all compassion, I worship you in the triune mystery of your mutual self-giving. Thank you for your love and care for all your creatures. Help me to live your love today, I pray. Amen.

✳ ✳ ✳

Cast all your anxiety on [the Lord], because he cares for you.

—1 Peter 5:7

WEDNESDAY

Dear Lord, thank you for your Word, written in Scripture and lived among us in Jesus Christ, the Living Word, and in all your saints. Continue to speak to me through your Word, made alive by your Spirit, and transform me by your truth, I pray. Amen.

✻ ✻ ✻

"Those who bring thanksgiving as their sacrifice honor me;
　　to those who go the right way
　　I will show the salvation of God."

—Psalm 50:23

THURSDAY

O Lord, I praise you that you delight to do good for your people. I worship you as your light widens over the horizon. Do your good work in and through me today, I pray. Help me honor you in all things, to the praise of your holy name. Amen.

✻ ✻ ✻

[Thus says the LORD,] They shall be my people, and I will be their God. I will give them one heart and one way, that they may fear me for all time, for their own good and the good of their children after them. . . . I will rejoice in doing good to them, and I will plant them in this land in faithfulness, with all my heart and all my soul.

—Jeremiah 32:38–39, 41

FRIDAY

O Lord God, my soul and my flesh cry out to you! I need your grace, guidance, and strength in all the hours ahead. I worship you and ask for your aid this day, through Jesus Christ, our Lord and Strength and Healer. Amen.

✳ ✳ ✳

> [My] heart and my flesh [cry] out for the living God.
> —Psalm 84:2 KJV

SATURDAY

O God, Lord of land and sea, skies and space, I worship you in awe and joy. Lord Jesus, I praise you for your plan of salvation and restoration. Holy Spirit, live in me and lead me in ways that glorify you this day, I pray. Amen.

✳ ✳ ✳

> I trust in the steadfast love of God
>   forever and ever.
> I will thank you forever,
>   because of what you have done.
>   —Psalm 52:8–9

Sunday

Holy God, Lord of time and history, I bow in awe before you on this day of reflection and rest. I recall your words about Sabbath and Jubilee and the restoration of all things. Lord Jesus, help me center my life fully in you, that I may share in your rest now and live actively in the hope of the realization of all you have promised, through the power of your Holy Spirit. Amen.

> "The Spirit of the Lord is upon me,
>   because he has anointed me
>   to bring good news to the poor.
> He has sent me to proclaim release to the captive
>   and recovery of sight to the blind,
>   to let the oppressed go free,
> to proclaim the year of the Lord's favor."
>
> —Jesus (Luke 4:18–19)

MONDAY

Holy Spirit, Wind of God, breathe on me today as I bow humbly and openly in your presence. Cleanse, fill, empower, and guide me this day, I pray. May Jesus Christ be exalted in my life, to the praise of your glorious grace. Amen.

❄ ❄ ❄

> I will extol you, my God and King,
> and bless your name forever and ever.
> Every day I will bless you,
> and praise your name forever and ever.
> Great is the LORD, and greatly to be praised;
> his greatness is unsearchable.
>
> —Psalm 145:1–3

TUESDAY

O Lord God! In vastness or minutiae; in things vital or things seemingly inconsequential, help me trust in you and be open to your Spirit. When trials come, help me by your Spirit to find them to be means of grace, I pray in Jesus' name as I praise you today. Amen.

❄ ❄ ❄

> One generation shall praise [your] works to another, and shall declare [your] mighty acts.
> I will speak of the glorious honour of [your] majesty, and of [your] wondrous works.
>
> —Psalm 145:4–5 KJV

WEDNESDAY

O God, I recognize that life is very complex—and that much of this complexity comes from your creative goodness, while much comes from human ingenuity, for good or ill. I commit all the diverse dimensions of my own life to you this day, Lord Jesus. Holy Spirit, align all the angles of my life and all my complexities and perplexities with your good kingdom purposes, I pray, that I may honor you in all things. Amen.

✳ ✳ ✳

The LORD is gracious and merciful,
  slow to anger and abounding in steadfast love.
The LORD is good to all,
  and his compassion is over all that he has made.
                                    —Psalm 145:8–9

THURSDAY

Blessed Jesus, loving Savior, I worship you and rest the full weight of my life, with all my duties, joys, and concerns, on you. Lord Jesus, be present in my life today by your Spirit, directing me in your good paths, I pray. Amen.

✳ ✳ ✳

Teach me, O LORD, the way of your statutes,
  and I will observe it to the end.
Give me understanding, that I may keep your law
  and observe it with my whole heart.
Lead me in the path of your commandments,
  for I delight in it.

                                    —Psalm 119:33–35

FRIDAY

O God, I set my hope and faith on the grace yet to be revealed in Jesus Christ. I thank you for the mighty work you have done in the life, death, and resurrection of Jesus, and for the resurrection power at work in me and in your church. Lord Jesus, live in me today. Reveal your grace, and make me an instrument of your reconciling work, through the power of the Holy Spirit, I pray. Amen.

Therefore prepare your minds for action; discipline yourselves; set all your hope on the grace that Jesus Christ will bring you when he is revealed.

—1 Peter 1:13

SATURDAY

Holy Lord God, I worship you today for your goodness, patience, purposefulness, and lovingkindness. Praise and glory be to you! Fill me with your love and praise this day, I pray, to the glory of your name. Amen.

> The LORD is faithful in all his words,
>   and gracious in all his deeds.
> The LORD upholds all who are falling,
>   and raises up all who are bowed down.
>   —Psalm 145:13–14

WEEK THIRTY-TWO

SUNDAY

Lord God, I trust in you; I worship you. Help me not to be so absorbed in the immediate concerns of my life that I miss your larger plans and purposes. Help me be faithful to you today as I rest in the certainty of your promises for all of history, for time and eternity, me included, I pray. Amen.

✳ ✳ ✳

The LORD is just in all his ways,
   and kind in all his doings.
The LORD is near to all who call on him,
   to all who call on him in truth.

—Psalm 145:17–18

Monday

O God, Blessed Trinity, I thank you that you have been working through the whole course of years and ages to accomplish your good purposes. Help me walk faithfully before you today, that I may fulfill my part in the long chain of your good providence, for the sake of future generations, I pray. Amen.

It is good for us to remember all the ways both of God's providence and grace, by which he has led us hitherto through the wilderness, that we may trust him, and cheerfully serve him.

—John Wesley, commentary on Deuteronomy 8:2
Explanatory Notes upon the Old Testament

Tuesday

O God, as I worship you and rejoice in your salvation, I remember that there is great suffering in the world—millions of people in prisons and in hospital beds and asylums; millions suffering from disease, oppression, torture, and absolute poverty. Lord God, be with them! Lord Jesus, may your kingdom come! Help me this day to live so that others may experience your liberation, I pray. Amen.

My mouth shall speak the praise of the Lord: and let all flesh bless his holy name for ever and ever.

—Psalm 145:21 KJV

WEDNESDAY

O Jesus, delight of my soul, I draw near you today in praise and love and rest. Thank you, precious Holy Spirit, for your grace in coming to me, waking me, and walking with me. Dear Lord, be with me in all I do today, to the glory of your name. I pray through Jesus Christ, our sure hope. Amen.

✳ ✳ ✳

The secret things belong unto the LORD our God: but those things which are revealed belong unto us and to our children for ever, that we may do all the words of this law.

—Deuteronomy 29:29 KJV

THURSDAY

Thank you, Sovereign Lord, for the sun, moon, and stars in their vast array. How many and wondrous are your works! Lord Jesus, be with me today, I pray, that I may live to praise you in your world. Amen.

✳ ✳ ✳

"There is no one like you, LORD, and there is no God but you, as we have heard with our own ears."

—1 Chronicles 17:20 NIV

FRIDAY

Jesus, Savior, Hope of the world, I worship you and long to see you known and honored among all peoples. Lord God, speed your Word today throughout the nations! May your kingdom come in new, fresh, and surprising ways in many places this day, I pray. Amen.

✳ ✳ ✳

"[T]he Lord searches every heart and understands every desire and every thought. If you seek him, he will be found by you; but if you forsake him, he will reject you forever."

—1 Chronicles 28:9 NIV

SATURDAY

Great God of time and un-time, I bow in loving submission to you at the rise of a new day. Holy Lord, since it is easy to be so absorbed by things of time and forget timeless realities, give me a true sense of the eternal, and of what that means for my life this very day, I pray. Amen.

✳ ✳ ✳

"Yours, O Lord, are the greatness, the power, the glory, the victory, and the majesty; for all that is in the heavens and on the earth is yours; yours is the kingdom, O Lord, and you are exalted as head above all."

—1 Chronicles 29:11

WEEK THIRTY-THREE

SUNDAY

God of peace and rest, I worship you this day and lay my life and labors at your feet. Lord Jesus, refresh my spirit and strengthen my resolve to serve and honor you in all things, I pray. All glory and praise be to you, Blessed Lord, Holy Trinity. Amen.

"In your hand are power and might; and it is in your hand to make great and to give strength to all. And now, our God, we give thanks to you and praise your glorious name."

—1 Chronicles 29:12–13

MONDAY

O Lord my God, I seek today to walk in your ways. I give myself anew to you and your purposes. Be glorified in all I think, do, and say, I pray, in the name of Jesus, my Savior, Example, Friend, and Guide. Amen.

✳ ✳ ✳

"I know, my God, that you search the heart, and take pleasure in uprightness. . . ."

—1 Chronicles 29:17

TUESDAY

Praise be to you, holy, loving, life-giving Lord. O God, I pray that you will renew and revive your church. Holy Spirit, breathe new life into the body of Christ, I pray. Fill me with your life and energy today, that I may be a means of genuine renewal and quickening, for the glory of your name and the healing of your world. Amen.

✳ ✳ ✳

The hand of the LORD came upon me, and he brought me out by the spirit of the LORD and set me down in the middle of a valley; it was full of bones. . . . He said to me, "Mortal, can these bones live?" I answered, "O Lord GOD, you know." Then he said to me, "Prophesy to these bones, and say to them: O dry bones, hear the word of the LORD. Thus says the Lord GOD to these bones: I will cause breath to enter you, and you shall live. I will lay sinews on you, and will cause flesh to come upon you, and cover you with skin, and put breath in you, and you shall live; and you shall know that I am the LORD."

—Ezekiel 37:1, 3–6

WEDNESDAY

O Lord God, source of strength, power, and healing, I come to you today in weakness and in need of your grace. Blessed Jesus, touch me by your Spirit. Give me strength and grace and health that I may faithfully serve you in all I do, to the glory of the Father. Amen.

✳ ✳ ✳

But surely, God is my helper;
the Lord is the upholder of my life.
—Psalm 54:4

THURSDAY

O God, my strength and joy, my hope and song are in you today. I acknowledge you as Lord and Savior. Help me to serve you, and strengthen me by your Spirit to love and honor you and be a faithful steward of your grace and your good land. Through Jesus Christ, I pray. Amen.

✳ ✳ ✳

For you have delivered my soul from death,
and my feet from falling,
so that I may walk before God
in the light of life.
—Psalm 56:13

FRIDAY

What wondrous love is this, Lord Jesus, that you willingly went to the cross for my sins and the sins of the world! Thank you, Lord, for your love and atonement. O Jesus, I love you and want to serve you faithfully in the power of the Holy Spirit. Show your love and grace and compassion in my life today, I pray. Amen.

✷ ✷ ✷

What happened on the cross was the self-expression of the love that made the world.

—N. T. Wright
The Day the Revolution Began

SATURDAY

Jesus, compassionate Savior, I worship you and give my life anew to your service. Help me to have the mind of Christ in all I do and say, I pray. May your Holy Spirit work in my life today that others may see Jesus, to the glory of the Father. Amen.

✷ ✷ ✷

I have one deep, supreme desire
That I may be like Jesus—
To this I fervently aspire,
That I may be like Jesus.
—Thomas O. Chisholm,
"I Want to Be Like Jesus"

WEEK THIRTY-FOUR

SUNDAY

Lord God, holy and loving Father, I praise and honor you today. Jesus Messiah, you who lived and laughed and suffered and won, be with me in my joys and struggles. Holy Spirit, graciously transform my every struggle and battle into a means of grace so that I may grow in grace and fruitful gospel faithfulness, I quietly pray. Amen.

❋ ❋ ❋

Be merciful to me, O God, be merciful to me,
    for in you my soul takes refuge;
in the shadow of your wings I will take refuge,
    until the destroying storms pass by.

—Psalm 57:1

MONDAY

Lord God, Blessed Trinity, I join with your people around the world in praising and honoring you today. Holy God, may your name be praised in *all* the nations. I give each moment of this day to you, to be lived to the praise of your glorious grace. Praise be to you, Lord Christ. Amen.

✳ ✳ ✳

> I cry to God Most High,
>   to God who fulfills his purpose for me.
> —Psalm 57:2

TUESDAY

O God, I thank you for the gospel of Jesus Christ, the power of God for the salvation of all who trust fully in you. I commit my way to you this day, asking that you would help me live your righteousness, that you may be glorified in my life and in your world. Amen.

✳ ✳ ✳

I am not ashamed of the gospel; it is the power of God for salvation to everyone who has faith, to the Jew first and also to the Greek.

—Romans 1:16

WEDNESDAY

O Lord, mighty God, as you acted in power to liberate Israel from Egyptian slavery, and brought salvation for all people through the blood of Jesus Christ, so I pray that today you would open the minds and hearts of people and nations to accept your saving, liberating work. Help me this day to serve you and be an agent of your grace, healing, and freeing power, I pray. Amen.

All the Israelites did just as the LORD had commanded Moses and Aaron. That very day the LORD brought the Israelites out of the land of Egypt, company by company.

—Exodus 12:50–51

THURSDAY

I praise you, O Lord, for your glorious grace—for all the ways you manifest your love and self-giving, and supremely for the grace of salvation through Jesus Christ by the Spirit. Work by your grace in my life today, and may I in all things be truly gracious. Amen.

Be exalted, O God, above the heavens;
let your glory be over all the earth.
—Psalm 57:5 NIV

FRIDAY

I thank you, Lord, that when I pray I do not pray alone, but with the deep help of your Spirit and in the company of saints and martyrs. Lord, I join my prayers and cries and intercessions with your faithful, godly people: May your kingdom come! May your will be done on earth as in heaven until the earth is "full of the knowledge of the LORD as the waters cover the sea" (Isa. 11:9). Amen.

Preaching the gospel and planting churches in the Carolinas in February 1789, Francis Asbury wrote: "I have ridden about one hundred and forty miles in the last seven days, through a very disagreeable part of the country to travel when the waters are high. I have had various exercises, and have suffered hunger, fatigue, and fever, and have not had a comfortable bed for a week past."

—The Journal and Letters of Francis Asbury

SATURDAY

Gracious God, I thank you for spring, with flowers and warm breezes and birds singing and rain falling. I praise you for new and renewed life. Help me walk with Jesus today, joyful in all you have made, and in deepening life in Christ through the Spirit, I pray. Amen.

"I know every bird in the mountains,
 and the insects in the fields are mine.
If I were hungry I would not tell you,
 for the world is mine, and all that is in it."
—Psalm 50:11–12 NIV

WEEK THIRTY-FIVE

SUNDAY

Thank you, O God, for the way of salvation, and that in your great plan "the leaves of the tree [of life] are for the healing of the nations." I live today in the hope and assurance of your salvation and your kingdom. Help me this day to honor you and be a sign of hope and healing to others. Amen.

✳ ✳ ✳

Then the angel showed me the river of the water of life, bright as crystal, flowing from the throne of God and of the Lamb through the middle of the street of the city. On either side of the river is the tree of life with its twelve kinds of fruit, producing its fruit each month; and the leaves of the tree are for the healing of the nations.

—Revelation 22:1–2

MONDAY

Lord, make me today an instrument of your peace. May I live your love and peace in all I do and say. Thank you for present peace and the promise of your *shalom* in the world. Be honored in my life, I pray. Amen.

✳ ✳ ✳

[Solomon said,] "O LORD, God of Israel, there is no God like you, in heaven or on earth, keeping covenant in steadfast love with your servants who walk before you with all their heart."

—2 Chronicles 6:14

TUESDAY

Lord God, Blessed Trinity, I exalt you today. I praise and honor you, seeking to worship you in the beauty of holiness and to serve you with all I am and all I have. Dear Father, may the beauty of Jesus be seen in me by the inward working of your Holy Spirit, I pray. Amen.

✳ ✳ ✳

[Solomon said,] "Regard your servant's prayer and his plea, O LORD my God, heeding the cry and the prayer that your servant prays to you."

—2 Chronicles 6:19

WEDNESDAY

O God, who led your people through the wilderness by a protecting pillar of cloud by day and fire by night, so lead your people today by Word and Spirit that your church may be your bright light to the nations. Dear Jesus, help me walk with you today in the light of your Word, by your Spirit, I pray. Amen.

They who make the glory of God their end, and the word of God their rule, the Spirit of God the guide of their affections, and the providence of God the guide of their affairs, may be confident that the Lord goes before them, as truly as he went before Israel in the wilderness.

—John Wesley, commentary on Exodus 13:21
Explanatory Notes upon the Old Testament

THURSDAY

Lord God of love, I praise you for the assurance that nothing can separate us from the love of God in Christ Jesus while we walk with you. Holy Spirit, actuate and guide me today in all I do, that I may abide in your presence and peace and be a means of your grace to others, I pray. Amen.

For I am convinced that neither death, nor life, nor angels, nor rulers, nor things present, nor things to come, nor powers, nor height, nor depth, nor anything else in all creation, will be able to separate us from the love of God in Christ Jesus our Lord.

—Romans 8:38-39

FRIDAY

Gracious Lord God, as all creation sings your praises, I would join my heart and voice in praise to you. Holy, Holy, Holy Lord; Blessed Father, Son, and Holy Spirit, all honor and glory be yours. I give my life to you and your service today, that your name may be praised throughout the earth. Amen.

❋ ❋ ❋

I will give thanks to you, O Lord, among the peoples;
  I will sing praises to you among the nations.
For your steadfast love is as high as the heavens;
  your faithfulness extends to the clouds.

—Psalm 57:9–10

SATURDAY

Spirit of life and power, as you have renewed and refreshed your people repeatedly in times past, I pray for your renewing work in the church today. O God, renew and revive your people, I pray. May the church be refreshed, and be your people and your witness in great faithfulness. Use me to this end, as you see fit, I pray. Amen.

❋ ❋ ❋

[The LORD said,] "If my people who are called by my name humble themselves, pray, seek my face, and turn from their wicked ways, then I will hear from heaven, and will forgive their sin and heal their land."

—2 Chronicles 7:14

WEEK THIRTY-SIX

SUNDAY

O God of love and kindness, thank you for the love of family and friends. Thank you for the heritage of parents and grandparents, and for the love of children and of brothers and sisters in the body of Christ. Blessed Holy Spirit, may I give and graciously receive your love today, I pray. Amen.

✳ ✳ ✳

This is the day that the LORD has made;
let us rejoice and be glad in it.
—Psalm 118:24

MONDAY

Blessed Trinity, God of truth and beauty and righteousness, I worship you and long to serve you faithfully today, with no deviation from your holy ways. Set a watch over my mind and imagination, that all I think and fleetingly imagine or ponder may align with your truth and love. I pray through Jesus Christ, the true Way. Amen.

❋ ❋ ❋

But I will sing of your might;
   I will sing aloud of your steadfast love in the morning.
For you have been a fortress for me
   and a refuge in the day of my distress.
O my strength, I will sing praises to you,
   for you, O God, are my fortress,
    the God who shows me steadfast love.

—Psalm 59:16–17

TUESDAY

Omnipresent God, blessed Holy Spirit, truly only you can renew your church and restore your fallen creation. My hope is in you. O God, act this day to bring new life to your church. Use me today, so that I may be a part of your renewing work, to the honor and praise of Jesus. All glory and honor be to you, Triune Lord. Amen.

❋ ❋ ❋

For God alone my soul waits in silence,
   for my hope is from him.
He alone is my rock and my salvation,
   my fortress; I shall not be shaken.
On God rests my deliverance and my honor;
   my mighty rock, my refuge is in God.

Trust in him at all times, O people;
   pour out your heart before him;
   God is a refuge for us.

—Psalm 62:5–8

WEDNESDAY

Lord God, who delivered Israel from Egypt in the exodus and formed a new people to serve you, I thank you for your work in Jesus Christ in forming your new people in the earth—the church, to be your witness and servant in the world. Thank you for the body of Christ. Help me to serve you through your body today, by the help of the Spirit, I pray. Amen.

> O God, you are my God, I seek you,
>   my soul thirsts for you;
> my flesh faints for you,
>   as in a dry and weary land where there is no water.
>
> —Psalm 63:1

THURSDAY

Holy Lord, loving Mother God, I bow in worship and love before you this day. Thank you for your compassion for all you have made. Fill me with your caring Spirit, I pray, that all I meet may know that you are love. Amen.

> He sympathized with hearts distressed,
> He spoke the words that cheered and blessed,
> He welcomed sinners to his breast—
> I want to be like Jesus!
>
> —Thomas O. Chisholm,
>   "I Want to Be Like Jesus"

FRIDAY

Jesus, Lord and Savior, constant friend, I quiet my heart and mind before you as night turns to light. Thank you for your help and strength over past days. O Jesus, help me walk faithfully with you today in the power of the Spirit, I pray, to the glory of the Father. Amen.

> For God alone my soul waits in silence;
>   from him comes my salvation.
> He alone is my rock and my salvation,
>   my fortress; I shall never be shaken.
>   —Psalm 62:1–2

SATURDAY

Loving, compassionate Lord, I hunger for a deeper, more constant communion with you; more of your presence by your Spirit in my life, moment by moment. Lead me deeper into the things of the Spirit, that I may be more fully like Jesus in the world, I pray. Amen.

> Because your steadfast love is better than life,
>   my lips will praise you.
> So I will bless you as long as I live;
>   I will lift up my hands and call on your name.
>   —Psalm 63:3–4

SUNDAY

Lord of justice, mercy, and truth, I worship you and bow humbly before you this day. I rest all I am and have and hope to be and do in you. Lord Jesus, help me by your Holy Spirit to do justice, love mercy, and walk in your truth, I pray. Amen.

[The Lord] has shown you, O mortal, what is good.
   And what does the LORD require of you?
To act justly and to love mercy
   and to walk humbly with your God.

—Micah 6:8 NIV

Monday

May all the nations praise you, O God; may all earth's peoples praise you! I exalt your name, gracious Lord, and give my life in your service. In your wise ecology, use me in some real way to spread your truth and grace through all the earth as I walk with you this day, I pray. Amen.

✴ ✴ ✴

By awesome deeds you answer us with deliverance,
    O God of our salvation;
you are the hope of all the ends of the earth
    and of the farthest seas.

—Psalm 65:5

Tuesday

O God, gracious Spirit, you have kindly opened to me many paths of ministry. I am not adequate for these things, but my hope and trust are in you. Dear Jesus, work in my life today; help me be a good steward of the grace you give me to minister for you and your kingdom, I pray. Amen.

✴ ✴ ✴

If I had cherished iniquity in my heart,
    the Lord would not have listened.
But truly God has listened;
    he has given heed to the words of my prayer.

Blessed be God,
    because he has not rejected my prayer
    or removed his steadfast love from me.

—Psalm 66:18–20

WEDNESDAY

O God of truth and love, I worship you for your lovingkindness and the deep treasures of your wisdom. Holy Spirit, inspire your church to "unite the pair so long disjoined, knowledge and vital piety." Lord Jesus, help me walk in your truth and passion and love today, I pray. Amen.

✳ ✳ ✳

Unite the pair so long disjoined,
Knowledge and vital piety:
Learning and holiness combined,
And truth and love, let all men see
In those whom up to thee we give,
Thine, wholly thine, to die and live.
—Charles Wesley, hymn for children. No. 473
A Collection of Hymns, For the Use of the People Called Methodists

THURSDAY

Just as the sun rises to give light and warmth to the new day, O Lord, I pray that you will rise in my heart, giving warmth and illumination to my path. Help me walk faithfully with you. Precious Jesus, shine through my life today by your Spirit, to the glory of the Father, I pray. Amen.

✳ ✳ ✳

Let the peoples praise you, O God;
let all the peoples praise you.

Let the nations be glad and sing for joy,
for you judge the peoples with equity
and guide the nations upon earth.
—Psalm 67:3–4

FRIDAY

Wise and holy God, Lord of the ages, I desire to be led today by you. My mind and heart, and all my days, are in your hands. Blessed Holy Spirit, lead me in the ways of Jesus and give me the mind of Christ in all I think and say, to the glory of the Father, I pray. Amen.

> But let the righteous be joyful;
>   let them exult before God;
>   let them be jubilant with joy.
> —Psalm 68:3

SATURDAY

O God, Blessed Trinity, I bow before you and adore your love, power, and holy communion. Praise and honor be to you, Father, Son, and life-giving Spirit. Fill me with your triune presence today, and help me to honor you in all I do and say, I pray. Amen.

> Sing to God, sing praises to his name;
>   lift up a song to him who rides upon the clouds—
> his name is the LORD—
>   be exultant before him.
>
> —Psalm 68:4

WEEK THIRTY-EIGHT

SUNDAY

Holy Spirit of God, I worship you now with all my heart, soul, mind, and imagination. Blessed Jesus, I want to please you today in all I say, think, and do. Praise and honor be to you, Holy Father. Please work in my life today that, from dawn to dark, this day may be one of constant praise and faithful service, I pray. Amen.

✽ ✽ ✽

Father of orphans and protector of widows
   is God in his holy habitation.
God gives the desolate a home to live in;
   he leads out the prisoners to prosperity,
   but the rebellious live in a parched land.
—Psalm 68:5–6

MONDAY

O God, blessed Trinity, I worship you and praise you that my life is hid with Christ in God. I want to please you all through this day and be a witness of your grace. Spirit of Jesus, work in my life today. Protect and keep me, and give me the compassionate eyes of Jesus, I pray. Amen.

❈ ❈ ❈

You are my hiding place;
   you will protect me from trouble
   and surround me with songs of deliverance.
                              —Psalm 32:7 NIV

TUESDAY

Lord God, blessed Trinity, I long to know you more deeply and to walk with you more wholly. As I renew my love and commitment at the rise of this day, I pray your Spirit will fill me deeply and dwell in me constantly till day's end. Blessed Jesus, be my life, my thought, my passion, and my peace, I pray. Amen.

❈ ❈ ❈

Blessed be the Lord,
   who daily bears us up;
   God is our salvation.
Our God is a God of salvation,
   and to GOD, the Lord, belongs escape from death.
                              —Psalm 68:19–20

WEDNESDAY

Holy Trinity, my Maker and my Provider, I bow in humble worship before you as this day wakens. O Lord, I would be wise in the things of God, in your ways and work and in your worship. Father God, help me to honor you in all I do and say, by the power of the Holy Spirit and to the service of Jesus Christ, I pray. Amen.

❉ ❉ ❉

A simple but often missed key to a disciplined life in the service of God: our time is limited, so every time we say yes to one thing, we say no to something else.

THURSDAY

O God, I aspire to love and honor and serve you today with my whole being—heart and mind, will and imagination, desire and decision. Praise and honor be to you, Lord Most High. Cleanse me today from every thought and image that would lead me away from you, and may my life be lived fully to your glory, I pray. Amen.

❉ ❉ ❉

We should allow no desire in our hearts, which we cannot in faith offer unto God by prayer.

—John Wesley, commentary on Deuteronomy 3:23
Explanatory Notes upon the Old Testament

FRIDAY

O God, I worship you today for your amazing saving grace. Glory and honor and praise be to you, precious Jesus, for your sacrifice for me and all humankind. I trust today in your atonement, and ask that by your Spirit I may be an instrument of your grace to others and your peace in the land, to the glory of the Father. Amen.

✳ ✳ ✳

> But as for me, my prayer is to you, O LORD.
>   At an acceptable time, O God,
>   in the abundance of your steadfast love, answer me.
> —Psalm 69:13

SATURDAY

Lord Jesus, I bow in wonder and praise before you at this timely yet timeless moment. I thank you for your plan for time and eternity; your unending, unbending purpose to reconcile and heal your whole creation. Lord God, help me to live this day in full harmony with your good purposes, I pray. Amen.

✳ ✳ ✳

> I will praise God's name in song
>   and glorify him with thanksgiving.
> —Psalm 69:30 NIV

SUNDAY

O God, I desire that all people everywhere—children, men and women, families and tribes and cities and nations, all lost and lonely ones—should know your love and peace. I worship you, blessed Jesus, Prince of Peace. May justice, mercy, and truth come quickly in the fullness of your kingdom. Help me this day, blessed Spirit, to walk in your love and peace and expectation. Amen.

✳ ✳ ✳

[When at last] God hath brought to light all the hidden things of darkness, whosoever were the actors therein, [it will] be seen that wise and good were all his ways; that he "saw through the thick cloud," and governed all things by the wise "counsel of his own will"; that nothing was left to chance or the caprice of men, but God disposed all "strongly and sweetly," and wrought all into one connected chain of justice, mercy, and truth.

—John Wesley, "The Great Assize," *Works*

MONDAY

Sovereign Lord of the universe, Holy Trinity, I lay my life before you this day, opening my heart, mind, and soul completely to you. Dear Lord, you know much better than I the depths of my heart and imagination and desire. Work in me by your Spirit that I may have a pure, undivided, devout heart in serving Jesus throughout this day, from beginning to end, I pray. Amen.

The LORD hears the needy,
    and does not despise his own that are in bonds.

Let heaven and earth praise him,
    the seas and everything that moves in them.
        —Psalm 69:33–34

TUESDAY

God of wisdom, of knowledge, of providential influence in human affairs, I bow in worship and submission before you this day. Lord God, help me trust fully in you for my own life and concerns, and for your larger purposes in history. Lord Jesus, live in me by your Spirit today, and increase my trust in your good purposes for me and all creation, I pray. Amen.

Let all who seek you
    rejoice and be glad in you.
Let those who love your salvation
    say evermore, "God is great!"
        —Psalm 70:4

WEDNESDAY

Holy Lord, who revealed yourself to Israel at Sinai and supremely to all the world through Jesus Christ, I worship you in humble gratitude this day. Lord God, I praise you for your plan of salvation and new creation. Help me now to serve you in the newness of your Spirit, I pray, and to the praise and honor of Jesus. Amen.

❉ ❉ ❉

In you, O Lord, I take refuge;
    let me never be put to shame.
In your righteousness deliver me and rescue me;
    incline your ear to me and save me.
Be to me a rock of refuge,
    a strong fortress, to save me,
    for you are my rock and my fortress.
                                        —Psalm 71:1–3

THURSDAY

All praise and honor be to you, holy, loving, saving Lord. I praise you for the power of your Spirit shown in the healing and conversion of many people in many lands today; for the worldwide growth of your church. Dear Jesus, help me faithfully to serve you and your church, local and global, to the glory of God the Father. Amen.

❉ ❉ ❉

But I will hope continually,
    and will praise you yet more and more.
My mouth will tell of your righteous acts,
    of your deeds of salvation all day long,
    though their number is past my knowledge.
                                        —Psalm 71:14–15

FRIDAY

Praise and honor be to you, Holy God, today, and through all ages. Today I give you myself—my life, my devotion, my energies, my intentions, my doubts. Blessed Holy Spirit, cleanse and empower and guide me now in every good path and purpose, in service to Jesus Christ and in praise to God the Father. Amen.

> I will instruct you and teach you the way you should go;
> I will counsel you with my eye upon you.
>
> —Psalm 32:8

SATURDAY

Blessed Word of God, I thank you that you became incarnate, taking on flesh and blood and pain that the whole world might be redeemed and healed. Precious Jesus, my trust and faith are in you this day, and all days. Holy Spirit, live and act in my life that the life of Jesus may be truly incarnate in all I do and say, I pray to the glory of God the Father. Amen.

> [The Lord] has pity on the weak and the needy,
> and saves the lives of the needy.
> From oppression and violence he redeems their life;
> and precious is their blood in his sight.
>
> —Psalm 72:13–14

WEEK FORTY

SUNDAY

Loving, all-seeing Spirit, as seasons change may your truth shine bright. As friends in the global south enter autumn, may they rest in you. As friends in the global north welcome springtime, may they awaken more and more to your grace. Lord God, who holds times and seasons in your hand, may the nations turn now to Jesus, the Sun of Justice and Righteousness, I pray. Amen.

At that time Jesus said, "I thank you, Father, Lord of heaven and earth, because you have hidden these things from the wise and the intelligent and have revealed them to infants; yes, Father, for such was your gracious will."

—Matthew 11:25–26

MONDAY

Living Lord Jesus, help me to be like Joseph of Arimathea, who was "waiting expectantly for the kingdom of God" and acted boldly. Holy Spirit, be my help and strength this day, I pray as I praise and walk the Jesus way. Amen.

✳ ✳ ✳

When evening had come, and since it was the day of Preparation, that is, the day before the sabbath, Joseph of Arimathea, a respected member of the council, who was also himself waiting expectantly for the kingdom of God, went boldly to Pilate and asked for the body of Jesus. . . . When [Pilate] learned from the centurion that [Jesus] was dead, he granted the body to Joseph.

—Mark 15:42–43, 45

TUESDAY

Lord Jesus, you call your disciples to be servants of others and stewards of the earth. You were among us as one who serves. Help me, Lord, to be a servant of you, other people, and your good creation, even when I would much rather serve myself or be served. Holy Spirit, make me a servant, I pray. May I be like Jesus today. Amen.

✳ ✳ ✳

You are my God, and I will give thanks to you;
you are my God, I will extol you.

O give thanks to the LORD, for he is good,
for his steadfast love endures forever.
—Psalm 118:28–29

WEDNESDAY

Holy God of love and grace, I worship you and open my heart to receive the grace you have for me today. Precious Jesus, fill me with your love. Blessed Holy Spirit, give me the mind of Christ, the compassion of God that sent Jesus into the world, I pray, that my life this day may be lived to your glory. Amen.

✹ ✹ ✹

Let my cry come before you, O LORD;
  give me understanding according to your word.
Let my supplication come before you;
  deliver me according to your promise.
—Psalm 119:169–70

THURSDAY

Lord Jesus, as you have said to love one another the way you loved your disciples, I open my heart to the ministry of your Spirit that you would pour your love more fully into my heart. Holy Spirit, love others through me today. Strengthen my compassion and care for all your disciples and for all earth's peoples, I pray. Amen.

✹ ✹ ✹

"I give you a new commandment, that you love one another. Just as I have loved you, you also should love one another. By this everyone will know that you are my disciples, if you have love for one another."
—Jesus (John 13:34–35)

FRIDAY

Lord Jesus, while on earth you were always devoted fully to doing the Father's will, little regarding what others thought. Help me this day to be focused on full obedience and devotion to you, not on what others think of me or on my own advancement. Lord Jesus, make me a true servant of you and your purposes, I pray. Amen.

Negligence will ruin us; but we cannot be saved without diligence.
—John Wesley, commentary on Deuteronomy 6:17
Explanatory Notes upon the Old Testament

SATURDAY

Holy Lord, Blessed Trinity, I join my heart and voice with your saints and angels in praising you this day. Truly heaven and earth are full of your glory! I worship you and praise you, Lord Most High. Lord Jesus, lead me in my life of service and praise by your Spirit, to the glory of God the Father, I pray. Amen.

My lips will pour forth praise,
    because you teach me your statutes.
My tongue will sing of your promise,
    for all your commandments are right.
—Psalm 119:171–72

WEEK FORTY-ONE

SUNDAY

Lord God, I thank you for the gift of free grace. Thank you for your self-giving for me and all your children, all your creation. Help me to receive and walk responsibly and responsively in your grace today, I pray. Amen.

✳ ✳ ✳

Let your hand be ready to help me,
    for I have chosen your precepts.
I long for your salvation, O LORD,
    and your law is my delight.
Let me live that I may praise you,
    and let your ordinances help me.
                  —Psalm 119:173–75

MONDAY

Holy Spirit of God, glory, honor, and praise be to you. I worship you and bow humbly before you. Work deeply in my spirit today that I may have the mind of Christ in all my thoughts, imaginations, and aspirations. Fill me with your love and regard for others, and deliver me from all jealousy when others succeed or surpass me in areas where I would like to excel or be known. Lord Jesus, give me a servant heart and spirit, I pray. Amen.

✻ ✻ ✻

I lift up my eyes to the hills—
    from where will my help come?
My help comes from the LORD,
    who made heaven and earth.

He will not let your foot be moved;
    he who keeps you will not slumber.
He who keeps Israel
    will neither slumber nor sleep.

—Psalm 121:1–4

TUESDAY

Lord God of peace and rest, I calm my heart before you as this day begins. Holy Spirit, I want to dwell in your quietness and calmness all day long, in all I do and say. Keep me, Lord Jesus, in your peace, and may I be a bearer of your peace to all I meet, I pray. Amen.

✻ ✻ ✻

The LORD is your keeper;
    the LORD is your shade at your
    right hand.
The sun shall not strike you by day,
    nor the moon by night.

The LORD will keep you from all evil;
    he will keep your life.
The LORD will keep
    your going out and your coming in
    from this time on and forevermore.

—Psalm 121:5–8

WEDNESDAY

O God, I worship you and sing your praise at the rise of this day. Holy, gracious, loving Lord, how great your power and compassion; how deep your wisdom and ways. Glory, honor, and praise be to you. Blessed Trinity, enable me to rightly sing your praise and righteously walk your ways, I pray. Amen.

> To you I lift up my eyes,
> O you who are enthroned in the heavens!
> As the eyes of servants
> look to the hand of their master,
> as the eyes of a maid
> to the hand of her mistress,
> so our eyes look to the LORD our God,
> until he has mercy upon us.
>
> —Psalm 123:1–2

THURSDAY

Lord Jesus, by your Word and example you showed us how to live, how to be your disciples. I want to walk faithfully today in your steps. Help me live a life of faithful discipleship that honors you, and to serve others in the Spirit of Jesus, I pray. Amen.

> Our help is in the name of the LORD,
> who made heaven and earth.
>
> —Psalm 124:8

FRIDAY

Thank you, Lord Jesus, for your love for me, for all your disciples, and for earth's scattered peoples. Thank you for sending the Comforter to live in your disciples, and in me. Holy, loving Spirit, teach me today to be a faithful follower of Jesus. Fill me with the Spirit of Jesus that I may dwell in you, and you in me, I pray. Amen.

"But the Advocate [or Comforter], the Holy Spirit, whom the Father will send in my name, will teach you everything, and remind you of all that I have said to you."

—Jesus (John 14:26)

SATURDAY

Lord Jesus, as you have said that you are the vine and your faithful disciples the branches, so I worship you, True Vine. I will to remain fruitfully, faithfully joined to you, Head and Body, today. As you have given the command to love one another, I pray your love will remain in me and your Spirit will love through me, that my life may be a fruitful extension of your love. Praise to you, Lord Jesus, source of life and love. Amen.

"I am the true vine, and my Father is the vinegrower. . . . I am the vine, you are the branches. Those who abide in me and I in them bear much fruit, because apart from me you can do nothing. . . . My Father is glorified by this, that you bear much fruit and become my disciples. As the Father has loved me, so I have loved you; abide in my love. . . .

"This is my commandment, that you love one another as I have loved you."

—Jesus (John 15:1, 5, 8–9, 12)

WEEK FORTY-TWO

SUNDAY

Dear Jesus, as when you walked this earth you were taught "what to say and how to say it," I pray that you would guide my words. Often I don't know just what to say. Holy Spirit, teach me today your words and your ways, that I may faithfully follow Jesus and live to the glory of the Father and the unveiling of your kingdom, I pray. Amen.

"I don't speak on my own authority. The Father who sent me has commanded me what to say and how to say it."

—Jesus (John 12:49 NLT)

MONDAY

Holy Lord, Blessed Trinity of love and self-giving, I worship you today and joy in your love for me and for your church and world. Lord Jesus, as you prayed that the love the Father has for you might be in your disciples, and that you yourself might be in them, I pray that I may this day be filled with your Holy Spirit of love, and that by your Spirit, Jesus' prayer for his church may be fully answered, to the glory of the Father. Amen.

✻ ✻ ✻

"Righteous Father, the world does not know you, but I know you; and these know that you have sent me. I made your name known to them, and I will make it known, so that the love with which you have loved me may be in them, and I in them."

—Jesus (John 17:25–26)

TUESDAY

O God, Sovereign Lord, I bow in your presence and acknowledge your reign over all things—over time, history, and eternity. Lord Jesus, may your kingdom come in all its fullness! Be exalted in my life today. In all I do and say, O Lord, may my purpose be to honor you, and may my life serve and reveal your kingdom, I pray. Amen.

✻ ✻ ✻

"My kingdom is not from this world. . ."

—Jesus (John 18:36)

WEDNESDAY

Jesus, Friend of sinners, I worship you and bow humbly before you as I begin a new day. Thank you, Lord Jesus, for your love to the last that led you to the cross so that all might be saved. Precious Lord, fill me with your love and compassion today. Help me love those you love, and do what you would have me do. Amen.

✣ ✣ ✣

Any person who thinks he or she is *controlled* by the Spirit is potentially dangerous. We are to be *guided* by the Spirit, and one fruit of this is self-control. Paul writes:

> The fruit of the Spirit is love, joy, peace, patience, kindness, generosity, faithfulness, gentleness, and self-control. . . . If we live by the Spirit, let us also be guided by the Spirit.
>
> —Galatians 5:22–23, 25

THURSDAY

Lord Jesus, you told your first disciples, "As the Father has sent me, so I send you." Thank you, Lord Jesus, for coming into the world at great cost to reveal the Father and show the way to life and holiness. Help me as one of your sent ones to be like Jesus today. Assist me by your Spirit to do my part so that the world may believe and have life in you, I pray. Amen.

✣ ✣ ✣

Then the disciples rejoiced when they saw the Lord. Jesus said to them again, "Peace be with you. As the Father has sent me, so I send you." When he had said this, he breathed on them and said to them, "Receive the Holy Spirit."

> —John 20:20–22

Friday

Sovereign Lord Jesus, who when you arose from the dead revealed yourself first to Mary Magdalene, I praise you for your love and self-revelation to the poor and weak and despised of the world. Truly you use the seemingly weak and foolish things to confound the wise and strong. Lord Jesus, I bow in weakness and self-emptying before you. Holy Spirit, be my strength this day, and reveal Jesus in and through me, to the glory of the Father, I pray. Amen.

✳ ✳ ✳

For God's foolishness is wiser than human wisdom, and God's weakness is stronger than human strength. . . .

God chose what is foolish in the world to shame the wise; God chose what is weak in the world to shame the strong; God chose what is low and despised in the world, things that are not, to reduce to nothing things that are, so that no one might boast in the presence of God.

—1 Corinthians 1:25, 27–29

Saturday

O God, Blessed Trinity of love, mercy, and truth, I worship you today in joy and praise, lifting my heart to you and giving myself anew to you and your service. High and holy and lovely one, glory and praise be yours this day and forevermore. Amen.

✳ ✳ ✳

May those who sow in tears reap with shouts of joy.
Those who go out weeping,
   bearing the seed for sowing,
shall come home with shouts of joy,
   carrying their sheaves.
                              —Psalm 126:5–6

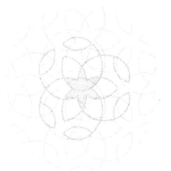

SUNDAY

Lord God of all things visible and invisible, your Word says we should honor you with our bodies as well as our minds and spirits. I give myself totally to you today, spirit and body. Incarnate Jesus, help me by your Spirit to live physically in the world in ways that please you, and to honor you in my stewardship of this material body you have crafted. To the glory of God the Father, I pray. Amen.

✳ ✳ ✳

Do you not know that your body is a temple of the Holy Spirit within you, which you have from God, and that you are not your own? For you were bought with a price; therefore glorify God in your body.

—1 Corinthians 6:19–20

MONDAY

Lord God of power and might and conquering love, you promise freedom to all who worship you in spirit and in truth. I bow humbly before you, Lord Jesus, opening my heart and mind to your guiding Spirit. Fill me with your fullness that I may walk in your freedom and love, to your glory and the fuller revealing of your kingdom in the world, I pray. Amen.

✻ ✻ ✻

> Out of the depths I cry to you, O LORD.
>   Lord, hear my voice!
> Let your ears be attentive
>   to the voice of my supplications!
>   —Psalm 130:1–2

TUESDAY

O God, I worship you and quiet my mind and spirit before you now. In the midst of many duties and responsibilities, O God, I desire to be found fully in Christ. Holy Spirit, be in all I do, think, and say this day, and keep me deeply, calmly in your peace. May I rest in you, O Father, and serve you with joy. Amen.

✻ ✻ ✻

> I wait for the LORD, my soul waits,
>   and in his word I hope;
> my soul waits for the Lord
>   more than those who watch for the morning,
>   more than those who watch for the morning.
>   —Psalm 130:5–6

WEDNESDAY

Lord God of grace and love, I thank you for your abundant provision for life in the world—for food and clothing; for shelter and safety; for family and significant work to do. Thank you, Lord Jesus. Help me be a faithful steward of all you give, that all I have and all I am may be always employed for the sake of your kingdom. Amen.

Praise the LORD, for the LORD is good;
  sing to his name, for he is gracious.
                              —Psalm 135:3

THURSDAY

Lord God of love, how broad and deep is your compassion, your care, and lovingkindness toward all people and all you have made. Loving God, I worship you and rest joyfully in your love. Holy Spirit, lead me deeper into the riches of divine love; make me more like Jesus in all I am and do and say, I pray, to the glory of God, Father, Son, and Holy Spirit. Amen.

O LORD, my heart is not lifted up,
  my eyes are not raised too high;
I do not occupy myself with things
  too great and too marvelous for me.
But I have calmed and quieted my soul,
  like a weaned child with its mother;
  my soul is like the weaned child that is with me.
                              —Psalm 131:1–2

FRIDAY

O God, Lord of life, as I praise you I pray: keep me centered in the center of the gospel. Holy Spirit, help me live the mind of Christ. Lord Jesus, fill me fully with your holy love. May I live a just and holy and joyful life, centered always in you, I pray. Amen.

> Make a joyful noise to God, all the earth;
>   sing the glory of his name;
>   give to him glorious praise.
> Say to God, "How awesome are your deeds!"
> —Psalm 66:1–3

SATURDAY

Thank you, Lord God, for the promise, and the frequent fulfillment throughout history, of "times of refreshing" from the Lord. Blessed Holy Spirit, grant again a renewal and refreshing to your church! Lord Jesus, live in my life today, that I may by your Spirit draw upon your gift of life and live in the refreshing dews of your Spirit, I pray. Amen.

In this way God fulfilled what he had foretold through all the prophets, that his Messiah would suffer. Repent therefore, and turn to God so that your sins may be wiped out, so that times of refreshing may come from the presence of the Lord, and that he may send the Messiah appointed for you, that is, Jesus, who must remain in heaven until the time of universal restoration that God announced long ago through his holy prophets.

> —Acts 3:18–21

WEEK FORTY-FOUR

SUNDAY

Lord God of eternity and time, I entrust my life anew into your hands. Keep me, Lord, this day, ready to live or die for you. I commit my way and open my heart fully to you in worship, Blessed Trinity, Father, Son, and Holy Spirit. Amen.

Death comes at all times, in all places, to all ages. We should live in constant readiness to exchange worlds.

—B. T. Roberts
"Death in a Church," *The Earnest Christian*

MONDAY

Lord God of truth, justice, and love, I thank you for the deep meaning of the cross demonstrated in the shocking death and surprising resurrection of Jesus. O Lord, help me live this day as a true disciple of Jesus and learn more fully the meaning of the cross for me, for your church, and for your kingdom, I pray. Amen.

❀ ❀ ❀

Christ is *agape;* self-giving, nonresistant love. . . . [Jesus' death on the cross] reveals how God deals with evil. . . . The cross is the extreme demonstration that *agape* seeks neither effectiveness nor justice, and is willing to suffer any loss or seeming defeat for the sake of obedience.

But the cross is not defeat. Christ's obedience unto death was crowned by the miracle of resurrection and the exaltation at the right hand of God.

—John Howard Yoder
The Original Revolution

TUESDAY

Lord God, Holy Trinity, I worship you and offer my life in praise and service for this day. Lord Jesus, strengthen me by your Holy Spirit, I pray, that my praise and my moment-by-moment life and obedience may be consistent, grounded in and empowered by you. Amen.

❀ ❀ ❀

We shall be owned [or acknowledged] and pronounced by God to be righteous and holy persons, if we sincerely obey him, otherwise we shall be declared to be unrighteous and ungodly.

John Wesley, commentary on Deuteronomy 6:25,
Explanatory Notes upon the Old Testament

WEDNESDAY

Lord God of love and unending redemptive energy, I thank you that you are making peace—peace in all dimensions and directions—through the blood of Jesus Christ, shed on the cross. I worship you, Blessed Lord, for your salvation—that which we now see and that yet to come. Holy Spirit, make me a walking sign of your peace this day, I pray. Amen.

Your name, O Lord, endures forever,
   your renown, O Lord, throughout all ages.
For the Lord will vindicate his people,
   and have compassion on his servants.
                              —Psalm 135:13–14

THURSDAY

Holy God, as I face another day, I recognize that I don't know all this day will bring. But my life and times are in your care. I worship you and newly commit my way to you. Holy, loving God, Blessed Trinity, guide me in your ways and be glorified in all I do and think and pray. I ask through Jesus Christ, our Lord. Amen.

O give thanks to the Lord, for he is good,
   for his steadfast love endures forever.
O give thanks to the God of gods,
   for his steadfast love endures forever.
O give thanks to the Lord of lords,
   for his steadfast love endures forever.
                              —Psalm 136:1–3

FRIDAY

Jesus, Lord and Savior, hope of the world and light of my life, I worship you and praise you this day. Lord Jesus, I once again commit all my way to you. Live in me today, that by your Spirit I may live your life before others, to the glory of the Father, I pray. Amen.

✻ ✻ ✻

Though the LORD is high, he regards the lowly;
but the haughty he perceives from far away.
—Psalm 138:6

SATURDAY

Dear Lord of grace and abundant love, I long to know you more deeply and serve you unfailingly. O God, increase my hunger and thirst for you, and fill me daily and deeply with your Holy Spirit. Thank you for your presence and your grace for this day. I pray through Jesus Christ, my life and my hope. Amen.

✻ ✻ ✻

The LORD will fulfill his purpose for me;
your steadfast love, O LORD, endures forever.
Do not forsake the work of your hands.
—Psalm 138:8

WEEK FORTY-FIVE

SUNDAY

O God, my life, I want to have the mind of Christ my Savior in all I do and say today. May my mind and heart be centered in you; may all my life in the world be an active testimony to your justice, mercy, and truth. Holy God, Blessed Savior, I worship you and praise you for your peace and presence this day. Amen.

✳ ✳ ✳

"Give justice to the weak and the orphan;
     maintain the right of the lowly and the destitute.
Rescue the weak and the needy;
     deliver them from the hand of the wicked."

—Psalm 82:3–4

Monday

Lord God of love and power, thank you in this holy hour for the abundant grace you give me. Thank you for your presence and power in my life. Father, help me today by your Holy Spirit to stand fast in your grace, and to walk in the holy ways of Jesus, I pray. Amen.

✳ ✳ ✳

But grow in the grace and knowledge of our Lord and Savior Jesus Christ. To him be the glory both now and to the day of eternity. Amen.

—2 Peter 3:18

Tuesday

Lord Jesus, precious Savior and Guide, I worship you and praise you and rest in you this day. Take my life and let it be consecrated, Lord, to you. I rejoice in your presence and commit myself anew to your purposes for me this day. Praise be to you, Lord God. Amen.

✳ ✳ ✳

Therefore, my brothers and sisters, whom I love and long for, my joy and crown, stand firm in the Lord in this way, my beloved.

—Philippians 4:1

WEDNESDAY

Thank you, Blessed Trinity, for the deep peace that comes through faith in Jesus, and through trusting you fully. Right now I renew my commitment to and trust in you, resting in you and your promises. Blessed Holy Spirit, work deeply in my life today, that my rest in Christ may equip me to serve you calmly and surely, to the glory of the Father. Amen.

For it was you who formed my inward parts;
   you knit me together in my mother's womb.
I praise you, for I am fearfully and wonderfully made.
   Wonderful are your works;
that I know very well.

—Psalm 139:13–14

THURSDAY

Lord God of love and grace, as so many of your purest saints have shown a tender love and sensitivity toward all the living creatures you have made, so may I this day be filled with compassion for all things living. May your love for all your matchless works stir up my solicitude for your creatures, great and small, I pray. Amen.

How weighty to me are your thoughts, O God!
   How vast is the sum of them!
I try to count them—they are more than the sand;
   I come to the end—I am still with you.

—Psalm 139:17–18

FRIDAY

Thank you, Lord, for the assurance this day that because you are God and Jesus is Lord, *all will be well*. This day, Lord, give me your grace, free me from all unholy distractions, and help me walk with you, led by the Spirit. I pray through Jesus, Lord, Savior, Healer, and Forerunner. Amen.

Search me, O God, and know my heart;
    test me and know my thoughts.
See if there is any wicked way in me,
    and lead me in the way everlasting.
            —Psalm 139:23–24

SATURDAY

Lord God, Holy Trinity, for the sake of your kingdom's coming on earth, assist me to serve you in ways that honor Jesus Christ and are led by your Spirit. Increase my faith and my fidelity, I pray. I worship you today with all my being. Amen.

I say to the LORD, "You are my God;
    give ear, O LORD, to the voice of my supplications."
            —Psalm 140:6

WEEK FORTY-SIX

SUNDAY

Lord God of Creation, I worship you now, your glory my passion and your kingdom my goal. Lead me by your Spirit in the way of Jesus as I listen and seek to serve you. Help me live a well-ordered life to your glory. Fill me with love and sure direction this day, I pray. Amen.

✳ ✳ ✳

I know that the LORD maintains the cause of the needy,
    and executes justice for the poor.
Surely the righteous shall give thanks to your name;
    the upright shall live in your presence.

—Psalm 140:12–13

MONDAY

O God, I trust in you and wait for you. I see that when I pray, good "coincidences" happen. When I don't, they don't. Dear Jesus, hear my prayers and intercessions and supplications today, I pray in faith and expectancy. Amen.

✵ ✵ ✵

But it is for you, O LORD, that I wait;
    it is you, O LORD my God, who will answer.
                  —Psalm 38:15

TUESDAY

Holy Spirit, I bow now in worship. Energize me to serve you today, I pray. I ask not that you rid me of my passions, but rather stir up all my passions for the sake of your glory and the coming of your kingdom. Fill me with your passionate love and truth today, for Jesus' sake. Amen.

✵ ✵ ✵

I call upon you, O LORD; come quickly to me;
    give ear to my voice when I call to you.
Let my prayer be counted as incense before you,
    and the lifting up of my hands as an evening sacrifice.
                  —Psalm 141:1–2

WEDNESDAY

Lord God,
May all I do, and all I say,
Bring glory to your name today.
Amen.

Set a guard over my mouth, O LORD;
keep watch over the door of my lips.
—Psalm 141:3

THURSDAY

Thank you, Lord, for birds and trees
And all the stars above—
Thank you for your presence near,
Thank you for your endless love.
Amen.

Every wild animal of the forest is mine,
the cattle on a thousand hills.
I know all the birds of the air,
and all that moves in the field is mine.
—Psalm 50:10–11

FRIDAY

Lord God of hope and guided happenings, be in all the serendipities of this day. May they be your good providences, I pray. Lead me by your Spirit; give me eyes to see and wise courage to serve you in serving others. This I gratefully pray. Amen.

✼ ✼ ✼

> But my eyes are turned toward you, O GOD, my Lord;
> in you I seek refuge; do not leave me defenseless.
>
> —Psalm 141:8

SATURDAY

O God, you who reveal yourself in many ways—in dreams and visions, in sacred Scriptures, in your holy creation, in circumstances, providences, and chance conversations—make me by your Spirit attentive to your voice. Thank you for revealing your grace and truth in Jesus Christ. Blessed Lord, help me walk in your ways today, I pray. Amen.

> With my voice I cry to the LORD;
> with my voice I make supplication to the LORD.
> I pour out my complaint before him;
> I tell my trouble before him.
> When my spirit is faint,
> you know my way.
>
> —Psalm 142:1–3

SUNDAY

Thank you, Lord, for your rest. Dear Jesus, help me live a wholesome blend of discipline and simple trust, rigor and rest, reverent fear and childlike confidence in you. Holy Spirit, grow in me the fruit of faith and good works, of sincere effort and peaceful calm, I pray. Amen.

❈ ❈ ❈

> I cry to you, O Lord;
>   I say, "You are my refuge,
>   my portion in the land of the living."
> —Psalm 142:5

MONDAY

Lord, it is a joy to walk with you. I renew my devotion to you today. Keep me so centered in you that my life is a prayer and a benediction to all I meet or touch along the way, I pray. Praise be to you! Amen.

✳ ✳ ✳

Praise the LORD!
Praise the LORD, O my soul!
I will praise the LORD as long as I live;
    I will sing praises to my God all my life long.
                                    —Psalm 146:1–2

TUESDAY

Lord, my joy is in you! Create in me a pure heart today. Keep me calmly in the profound simplicity of your grace, I pray. Amen.

✳ ✳ ✳

Happy are those whose help is the God of Jacob,
    whose hope is in the LORD their God,
who made heaven and earth,
    the sea, and all that is in them;
who keeps faith forever;
    who executes justice for the oppressed;
    who gives food to the hungry.

                                    —Psalm 146:5–7

WEDNESDAY

O Lord my God, when I am filled with uncertainties, questions, or doubts, help me trust fully in you. Hold me securely in your grace, I pray, through the power of the Risen One. Amen.

The LORD sets the prisoners free;
    the LORD opens the eyes of the blind.
The LORD lifts up those who are bowed down;
    the LORD loves the righteous.
The LORD watches over the strangers;
    he upholds the orphan and the widow,
    but the way of the wicked he brings to ruin.
                                        —Psalm 146:7–9

THURSDAY

When I consider vastness, O Lord—the universe, the intricacies of creation, the depths of the human heart and imagination—I turn to you in hope with my questions and wonderings. Holy Lord, I rest today in the vastness of your love and wisdom and power. Holy Spirit, help me trust fully in you this day, I pray. Amen.

Praise the LORD!
How good it is to sing praises to our God;
    for he is gracious, and a song of praise is fitting.
                                        —Psalm 147:1

FRIDAY

How beautiful, O Lord, how beautiful you are in yourself and in your manifestation in your works and wonders! I worship humbly before you, trusting your Spirit to guide and sustain me today in seeking to serve you. Praise be to you, Lord God. Amen.

✳ ✳ ✳

He determines the number of the stars;
   he gives to all of them their names.
Great is our Lord, and abundant in power;
   his understanding is beyond measure.
            —Psalm 147:4–5

SATURDAY

Lord God of time and eternity, of creation made, preserved, and restored, I pause now to ponder and to praise. Praying, "Holy, Holy, Holy," I realize the day is coming when I will see you face-to-face as I enter New Creation in fullness. So help me live now that I may meet you in joy and flourish in the new earth and heaven to your glory, I pray. Amen.

✳ ✳ ✳

So be careful not to forget the covenant that the LORD your God made with you . . . For the LORD your God is a devouring fire, a jealous God.
            —Deuteronomy 4:23–24

WEEK FORTY-EIGHT

SUNDAY

Dear Lord, I bow before you in worship and praise. Fill me body, mind, and spirit for this day. Strengthen and give health of body, clarify and enlighten my mind, warm my heart and inflame me with your outreaching love, I pray. Amen.

Bless the LORD, O you his angels,
　　you mighty ones who do his bidding,
　　obedient to his spoken word.
Bless the LORD, all his hosts,
　　his ministers that do his will.
Bless the LORD, all his works,
　　in all places of his dominion.
Bless the LORD, O my soul.
　　　　　　　　　—Psalm 103:20–22

MONDAY

Holy Lord, full of lovingkindness, I gladly worship you this day. May your kingdom come! Holy Spirit, send a great awakening, a great kingdom-of-God revival, according to your will, wisdom, and way. Lord Jesus, keep me open to your big and little works in my life today, to the praise of your glorious grace, I pray. Amen.

> [The Lord] covers the heavens with clouds,
>   prepares rain for the earth,
>   makes grass grow on the hills.
> He gives to the animals their food,
>   and to the young ravens when they cry.
> —Psalm 147:8–9

TUESDAY

O Lord, give me evermore the spirit and mind of Mary: "Here I am, the servant of the Lord; let it be with me according to your word." Amen.

The angel [Gabriel] said to her, "The Holy Spirit will come upon you, and the power of the Most High will overshadow you; therefore the child to be born will be holy; he will be called Son of God. And now, your relative Elizabeth in her old age has also conceived a son; and this is the sixth month for her who was said to be barren. For nothing will be impossible with God." Then Mary said, "Here am I, the servant of the Lord; let it be with me according to your word."

—Luke 1:35–38

WEDNESDAY

O Lord God of compassion, I am deeply troubled by the widespread suffering and pain in your world. I think of those in prison; people being tortured; children suffering abuse; people in lonely agony with none to help; women and children dying of famine. Help, Lord! Come in justice and mercy. Show me my healing work today, and may your kingdom come quickly, ending all wrong and injustice, I pray. Amen.

[You O Lord] have been a refuge to the poor,
   a refuge to the needy in their distress,
   a shelter from the rainstorm and a shade from the heat.
—Isaiah 25:4

THURSDAY

O God, you know my heart. You know that my love for you is sincere, even if weak; and my walk with you is determined, even if stumbling. Strengthen me by your Spirit to walk in your ways and love as Jesus loved, I pray. Amen.

God is our refuge and strength,
   a very present help in trouble.
Therefore we will not fear, though the earth should change,
   though the mountains shake in the heart of the sea;
though its waters roar and foam,
   though the mountains tremble with its tumult.
—Psalm 46:1–3

FRIDAY

Loving Father, thank you for the gift of Jesus and the mysterious moving of your Spirit. Touch me today in body, mind, and spirit that I may be entirely and integrally yours and given to you and your good purposes, I pray. Amen.

✳ ✳ ✳

"For the LORD your God is gracious and merciful, and will not turn away his face from you, if you return to him."

—2 Chronicles 30:9

SATURDAY

Lord God, thank you for the coming of Jesus—for the fear-shattering "good news of great joy for all the people" and the revelation of the life that was and is and shall be "the light of all people." Amen.

✳ ✳ ✳

But the angel said to them, "Do not be afraid; for see—I am bringing you good news of great joy for all the people."

—Luke 2:10

All things came into being through him, and without him not one thing came into being. What has come into being in him was life, and the life was the light of all people.

—John 1:3–4

WEEK FORTY-NINE

SUNDAY

Holy Lord, if you speak to me through the written Word, revealing your love in Jesus and the wonder of your salvation—or if you speak to me in your amazingly complex Book of Nature, showing your wisdom, power, and glory—either or both, I praise you and seek by your Spirit to learn and walk in your ways. Amen.

✳ ✳ ✳

Ever since the creation of the world [God's] eternal power and divine nature, invisible though they are, have been understood and seen through the things he has made.

—Romans 1:20

MONDAY

O Lord, in times when when many people are in love with the *idea* of Jesus Christ but not really interested in discipleship, help me be a true and faithful follower of the Savior. By Spirit and Word make me a doer of the Word and not a hearer only, I pray. Amen.

✻ ✻ ✻

Be doers of the word, and not merely hearers who deceive themselves. For if any are hearers of the word and not doers, they are like those who look at themselves in a mirror; for they look at themselves and, on going away, immediately forget what they were like. But those who look into the perfect law, the law of liberty, and persevere, being not hearers who forget but doers who act—they will be blessed in their doing.

—James 1:22–25

TUESDAY

O God, Sovereign Spirit, the ways my little life connects with your vast kingdom project are largely hidden to me, yet by faith I know they are joined. May I honor and serve you today, and may your kingdom come, I pray in Jesus' name. Amen.

✻ ✻ ✻

The LORD has established his throne in the heavens,
   and his kingdom rules over all.

—Psalm 103:19

WEDNESDAY

Discerning Spirit, in an age when politicians, pundits, and even many Christians split the world into right or left, liberal or conservative, graciously give me the radical mind of King Jesus. Remind me that the wisdom of this world is foolishness in kingdom perspective, and that you use the weak, despised things of this world to shame the strong. Amen.

✳ ✳ ✳

Praise the LORD!
Praise God in his sanctuary;
   praise him in his mighty firmament!
Praise him for his mighty deeds;
   praise him according to his surpassing greatness!
      —Psalm 150:1–2

THURSDAY

I praise you, Holy Lord, for your love and grace and constant providence. Lord Jesus, I pray you will infect your church with a renewed and expanding vision of the kingdom of God. May your kingdom come, O Lord, according to your good purposes and promises, whether or not that matches our hopes and expectations. Come, Holy Spirit, and renew the face of the earth. Amen.

✳ ✳ ✳

Seraphs were in attendance above him; each had six wings: with two they covered their faces, and with two they covered their feet, and with two they flew. And one called to another and said:

"Holy, holy, holy is the LORD of hosts;
the whole earth is full of his glory."

      —Isaiah 6:2–3

FRIDAY

Holy Lord of gardens and trees—of Eden and Olivet, Gethsemane, New Jerusalem—I worship you in and through your green creation in its beauty and agony and promise. O Lord, work your work, fulfill your plan, redeem your world quickly, I pray, as I wait patiently for you and for Jesus fully to be revealed. Amen.

Let everything that breathes praise the LORD!
Praise the LORD!

—Psalm 150:6

SATURDAY

Lord, I am deeply conscious of your grace and compassion. Help me to remember also your justice and judgment, I pray, so that my trust does not become presumption or melt into cheap grace. Still, "in wrath may you remember mercy." Let me live and rest in your truth. Amen.

O LORD, I have heard of your renown,
and I stand in awe, O LORD, of your work.
In our own time revive it;
in our own time make it known;
in wrath may you remember mercy.

—Habakkuk 3:2

WEEK FIFTY

SUNDAY

Lord God, Blessed Holy Spirit, may your Word be interpreted properly in your church. Banish wrong teachings; expel false ideologies and alien doctrines. O Jesus, living Word, reveal yourself by your Spirit through the Scriptures in fresh and faithful ways, I pray, for you assure us that the Scriptures testify of you. Amen.

✵ ✵ ✵

"The works that the Father has given me to complete, the very works that I am doing, testify on my behalf that the Father has sent me. And the Father who sent me has himself testified on my behalf. . . .

You search the scriptures because you think that in them you have eternal life; and it is they that testify on my behalf."

—Jesus (John 5:36–37, 39)

MONDAY

Lord God of holy love and potent compassion, move among us in convicting power, I pray. Holy Lord, please send a great Holy Ghost, kingdom-of-God, nation-shaking, shalom-bringing revival. Work today in my life in ways consistent with your larger purposes, I pray. Amen.

"Come, let us return to the LORD;
for it is he who has torn, and he will heal us;
he has struck down, and he will bind us up.
After two days he will revive us;
on the third day he will raise us up,
that we may live before him."

—Hosea 6:1–2

TUESDAY

Help me, Lord Jesus, in the great adventure of life and living, always to center my life in you—you, indwelling Savior, who also stand behind me, walk before me, and watch over me and your world by your providential Holy Spirit. All praise, honor, and joyful blessing be to you, Holy God, this day and forever. Amen.

"Do not fear those who kill the body but cannot kill the soul; rather fear him who can destroy both soul and body in hell. Are not two sparrows sold for a penny? Yet not one of them will fall to the ground apart from your Father. And even the hairs of your head are all counted. So do not be afraid; you are of more value than many sparrows."

—Jesus (Matthew 10:28–31)

WEDNESDAY

O Lord, Holy One, I find *time* itself to be a mystery. Sequence and consequence march on, whatever I do or fail to do. Thank you that time and all times are in your hands, and that your good purposes are sure, within time and beyond. May I steward well the time and grace allotted me, I pray. Amen.

✻ ✻ ✻

"Those who find their life will lose it, and those who lose their life for my sake will find it."

—Jesus (Matthew 10:39)

THURSDAY

O Lord, even as I worship you and seek to serve you, I know I am vulnerable to self-deception. So I commit myself fully, body and spirit, conscious and unconscious mind, into your hands. Purify my thoughts and intentions and imaginations, and work in all my life today, I pray. Amen.

✻ ✻ ✻

The Holy Spirit, by removing prejudice, by rooting out the selfishness of the heart, makes reason more reliable. . . .

One can be led by the *Spirit,* and at the same time exercise the strongest good sense, the soundest judgment. "The meek will he guide in judgment" (Ps. 25:9).

—B. T. Roberts
"Led by the Spirit," *The Earnest Christian*

FRIDAY

Lord God of wisdom, truth, and holiness, hear my prayer as I praise and worship you. I may see many things and be seen by many people today. Help me to remember that above all I live in your sight and walk before you, in your full view. Amen.

✦ ✦ ✦

"For the eyes of the LORD range throughout the entire earth, to strengthen those whose heart is true to him."

—2 Chronicles 16:9

SATURDAY

Sovereign Lord, you tell us the whole earth is full of your glory. Yet often I fail to see how this is so. Please make me like Elisha's servant, whose eyes were opened to see the armies of the Lord filling the hills all around. Help us walk daily in the light of your glory, I pray. Amen.

✦ ✦ ✦

Then Elisha prayed: "O LORD, please open his eyes that he may see." So the LORD opened the eyes of the servant, and he saw; the mountain was full of horses and chariots of fire all around Elisha.

—2 Kings 6:17

WEEK FIFTY-ONE

SUNDAY

Lord God of truth, I worship you! Please keep me today from heedless and needless self-indulgence. May I be disciplined in my walk with you, and in all I do. Form Jesus' steadfast, purposeful character in me by your Spirit and through your body, the church, I pray. Amen.

✻ ✻ ✻

But the steadfast love of the LORD is from everlasting to everlasting
   on those who fear him,
   and his righteousness to children's children,
to those who keep his covenant
   and remember to do his commandments.

—Psalm 103:17–18

MONDAY

Thank you, Lord, our Father and Mother, our Savior and Provider, ancient promise-maker and sure promise-keeper, for the good news of salvation and restoration through Jesus Christ. Holy Spirit, work in our hearts and lives so that your kingdom becomes increasingly visible in the world today, I pray. Amen.

✳ ✳ ✳

"Come to me, all you that are weary and are carrying heavy burdens, and I will give you rest. Take my yoke upon you, and learn from me; for I am gentle and humble in heart, and you will find rest for your souls. For my yoke is easy, and my burden is light."

—Jesus (Matthew 11:28–30)

TUESDAY

God of wisdom, hear my prayer. In all my learning, may I learn your truth. In all my thinking, may I think of you. In all my doing, may my walk be true. In all my speaking, may my words be kind. In all my spending—time, energy, money, attention—may I faithfully steward your grace here in your world, I pray. Amen.

✳ ✳ ✳

Therefore, my beloved, be steadfast, immovable, always excelling in the work of the Lord, because you know that in the Lord your labor is not in vain.

— 1 Corinthians 15:58

WEDNESDAY

O God, when I am all caught up in the tension or terror of the present moment, remind me of your past presence and the certainty of your future help and your unshakable promises. Give me the rest and peace that transcend time, I pray. I worship you today. Amen.

"All things have been handed over to me by my Father; and no one knows the Son except the Father, and no one knows the Father except the Son and anyone to whom the Son chooses to reveal him."

—Jesus (Matthew 11:27)

THURSDAY

All praise be yours, Holy Three-in-One God! Blessed Father, awaken the church and the nations to your fiery holiness and your wrath toward sin. O Jesus, reveal your grace and transforming love in new ways today. Holy Spirit, convict us of our godlessness and self-focus and spiritual blindness. Awaken your church and remake your wandering world, I pray. Amen.

"Here is my servant, whom I have chosen,
   my beloved, with whom my soul is well pleased.
I will put my Spirit upon him,
   and he will proclaim justice to the Gentiles. . . .
He will not break a bruised reed
   or quench a smoldering wick
until he brings justice to victory."

—Matthew 12:18, 20

FRIDAY

Sovereign Spirit, as you have firmly promised that the earth will be full of the knowledge of the Lord as the waters cover the sea, so expand my hope and vision that my life may be a true if small sign that your promises are unshakable, I pray. Amen.

❋ ❋ ❋

The wolf shall live with the lamb,
  the leopard shall lie down with
      the kid,
the calf and the lion and the fatling
  together,
  and a little child shall lead them.
The cow and the bear shall graze,
  their young shall lie down together;
  and the lion shall eat straw like the ox.

The nursing child shall play over the
  hole of the asp,
    and the weaned child shall put its
      hand on the adder's den.
They will not hurt or destroy
  on all my holy mountain;
for the earth will be full of the knowledge
  of the LORD
  as the waters cover the sea.

—Isaiah 11:6–9

SATURDAY

O Lord, open the wisdom of your written Word to me daily, more and more. Give me that godly wisdom and perspective that come solely from you, so that I can freely dismiss all the distracting, misleading messages that constantly call to us through worldly media. Teach me your ways, O Lord, Living Word, Holy Spirit. Amen.

❋ ❋ ❋

"For whoever does the will of my Father in heaven is my brother and sister and mother."

—Jesus (Matthew 12:50)

WEEK FIFTY-TWO

SUNDAY

Great God of the universe, I pray that small as I am, weak as I am, ignorant as I am, my life may this day in some way by grace be strategic for the coming of your kingdom on earth. In Jesus by the Spirit, I pray. Amen.

"But as for what was sown on good soil, this is the one who hears the word and understands it, who indeed bears fruit and yields, in one case a hundredfold, in another sixty, and in another thirty."

—Jesus (Matthew 13:23)

MONDAY

Jesus, perfect Savior, I worship you today. When I am discouraged with myself for not being more like you, remind me of your promise to be in me and with me forever. Help me draw closer to my brothers and sisters in Christ, not to withdraw into myself, I pray. Strengthen me by your Spirit. Amen.

✳ ✳ ✳

[Jesus] put before them another parable: "The kingdom of heaven is like a mustard seed that someone took and sowed in his field; it is the smallest of all the seeds, but when it has grown it is the greatest of shrubs and becomes a tree, so that the birds of the air come and make nests in its branches."

—Matthew 13:31–32

TUESDAY

Holy, Holy, Holy Lord God of the heavenly realms! Surely the whole earth is full of your glory. Lord of justice and covenant, fortify my faith and fidelity this day. May I may honor you, walk in your ways, and fulfill the vocation you give me and all your people, I pray. Amen.

✳ ✳ ✳

The LORD of hosts is with us;
the God of Jacob is our refuge.
—Psalm 46:11

WEDNESDAY

Today I praise you, Holy Father, Risen Jesus, Guiding Holy Spirit. Dear Lord, help me today. Use the struggles, pains, questions, or frustrations of this day to build steadfast character and Christlikeness in me, I pray. Amen.

※ ※ ※

[Jesus] told them another parable: "The kingdom of heaven is like yeast that a woman took and mixed in with three measures of flour until all of it was leavened."

—Matthew 13:33

THURSDAY

Lord God, as I begin this day with you, I draw all the scattered lines of thought and care together in focus on you, your love, your subtle guidance, your calm. I rest in you. "When the cares of my heart are many, your consolations cheer my soul" (Ps. 94:19). Praise and honor be yours today, Lord Jesus. Amen.

※ ※ ※

"Then the righteous will shine like the sun in the kingdom of their Father. Let anyone with ears listen!"

—Jesus (Matthew 13:43)

FRIDAY

Loving Lord God, I worship you. Amid the jumble of concerns, preoccupations, conflicts, and confusions of life, send today your discerning Spirit, I pray, that I may rest in you, trust you, and perceive you acting in my life and in your conflicted world. Amen.

"Therefore every scribe who has been trained for the kingdom of heaven is like the master of a household who brings out of his treasure what is new and what is old."

—Jesus (Matthew 13:52)

SATURDAY

Lord God, Sovereign Creator, Master of worlds, I bow my heart in awe-filled worship. In difficult days, help me trust fully in you. Lord Jesus, may I never lose the vision of your kingdom. Holy Spirit, let not our hope fade or the vision of all creation healed grow dim. Help me walk faithfully, hopefully, confidently in your ways today and be a bearer of good news, I pray. Amen.

And early in the morning [Jesus] came walking toward them on the sea. But when the disciples saw him walking on the sea, they were terrified, saying, "It is a ghost!" And they cried out in fear. But immediately Jesus spoke to them and said, "Take heart, it is I; do not be afraid."

—Matthew 14:25–27

SPECIAL DAYS OF
THE CHRISTIAN YEAR

FIRST SUNDAY OF ADVENT

Gracious Father, in this Advent season please give your church a new openness, a new sensitivity, a new receptivity to your truth, your Spirit, your transforming power—to the true and only Messiah. Hear our prayer, O Lord. Amen.

✳ ✳ ✳

CHRISTMAS DAY

Lord God of time, history, and redemption, thank you for the coming of Jesus, the one who takes away the sin of the world. As we sing of "fields and floods, rocks, hills, and plains" repeating "the sounding joy" of Jesus' reign, so may we today join all creation in praising you and partnering in your mission. Amen.

✳ ✳ ✳

DECEMBER 31

Blessed Trinity of love—Father, Son, and Holy Spirit—I rest in you as this year's last moments drift into history. Holy Lord, I worship you with mind and heart, trusting both past and future into your sure hands, with thanksgiving and boundless biblical hope. Amen.

✳ ✳ ✳

ASH WEDNESDAY (BEGINNING OF LENT)

Righteous Lord, as today I pause to reflect, please speak to me through your Word. May it never lose its sharpness. May I not insulate my heart from its piercing truth or become callous to its call to radical discipleship.

I pray through the living, self-giving Word, Jesus Christ, who still speaks today. Amen.

✳ ✳ ✳

FIRST SUNDAY IN LENT

Lord God, just now I hold up all my priorities, passions, and responsibilities before you. Lord Jesus, help me sort them out according to your priorities and passions. In all things may I seek first your glory and embody your kingdom, I pray, by the help of your Spirit. Amen.

✳ ✳ ✳

PALM SUNDAY

Praise to you, King Jesus! O Lord, your Word tells us "the whole earth is full of [your] glory" (Isa. 6:3). As I worship you and walk in your world today, give me eyes to see your glory, and to see the ways you want to reveal yourself through me. Where your glory is obscured, send your light and give sight to the blind, I pray. Amen.

✳ ✳ ✳

GOOD FRIDAY

Mortal Lord Jesus, who died with the weight of the world on your shoulders and the sin of humanity on your heart, sharper than nail or thorn or spear, I bow in thankfulness before you. Thank you for your sacrifice; your atoning death on the cross; and that "it was impossible for death to keep its hold" on you (Acts 2:24 NIV), Word made flesh. Glory be to the Father, to the Son, and to the Holy Spirit. Amen.

✳ ✳ ✳

EASTER SUNDAY (1)

Thank you, Risen Lord Jesus, that in your resurrection you are fulfilling everything written about you in the Law, the Prophets, and the Psalms (see Luke 24:44). I praise you for your resurrection—its historic reality and the guarantee it gives for our own resurrection and the restoration of all creation. Glory be to the Father, the Son, and the Holy Spirit, world without end. Amen.

✳ ✳ ✳

EASTER SUNDAY (2)

Blessed Jesus, Risen One, I rejoice today in your resurrection. I praise you for your victory over sin and death, and that the same power that raised you from the dead is still at work in your church. Renew your church to new life, I pray, and use me in the service of your body. Amen.

✳ ✳ ✳

PENTECOST SUNDAY

Blessed Holy Spirit, who even now breathes and broods over your church and the whole creation, I worship you today. Spirit of life, renew your church, and breathe fresh energy into my life, that I may live like Jesus, I pray. Amen.

✳ ✳ ✳

ALL SAINTS' DAY (NOVEMBER 1)

O God, your faithful servants have suffered and persevered as they served you throughout the years. Thank you for all saints and martyrs who have gone before. Help me by your Spirit to be your steadfast servant and witness in all I do this day, I pray through our Lord and Savior, Jesus Christ, who endured the cross and was made "perfect through sufferings" (Heb. 2:10). Amen.

✳ ✳ ✳

PRAYERS FOR SPECIAL SITUATIONS OR CIRCUMSTANCES

START OF A BUSY WEEK

Lord Jesus, today starts another very busy week. I need your wisdom, energy, and strength. Fill me with your Spirit that I may walk as a true Christian. Give me clear thought, determination, sensitivity to those around me, deep wisdom, and in all things the Spirit of Jesus, I pray. Amen.

※ ※ ※

A BIRTHDAY PRAYER

I praise you, O Lord, for your grace and presence with me over past years. These have been good years; an adventure, years of growth in knowing you and understanding your ways. Yet I sense my weakness and great dependence on you. May I truly grow from glory to glory through my remaining years so that when the time comes to move from this life to the next, it may be a small step. I love you today. Amen.

※ ※ ※

THANKSGIVING FOR FAMILY

I thank you, O God, for the blessing of parents who loved me, taught me your Word, introduced me to your people, and helped me come to know you. Thank you for these and other early blessings and influences that led me to you. Lord Jesus, help me this day to serve you faithfully and be a true example to others of your grace and truth, I pray. Amen.

✴ ✴ ✴

WHEN I MAKE A MISTAKE

O Lord, I goofed again. I made a dumb mistake. I am sorry, and ask that your goodness and grace may strengthen me this day that I may walk in truth and holiness and the love of Jesus. Amen.

✴ ✴ ✴

WHEN DEPRESSED

Lord God of compassion, Spirit of love, help me in times of deepest depression to know that even deeper are your everlasting arms. Hold me steady when I feel like letting go, and help me know that great is your faithfulness. Amen.

✴ ✴ ✴

WHEN DISTRESSED

O God, when in darkness the tangle of many thoughts and unresolved tensions invade my mind, even disturbing my sleep, surround me by your Spirit and lift me newly into your rest. I commit all to you and trust humbly in you. Bring my spirit back repeatedly to its one true rest, I pray with joy in your promises. Amen.

✴ ✴ ✴

WHEN BURDENED WITH DUTIES

Lord God of wisdom, when I feel the weight of responsibilities or decisions, help me to be not anxious, but creative. Work through me, and in spite of me, for your good purposes, I pray. I trust in you. Amen.

✴ ✴ ✴

WHEN WORRIED OR WEIGHED DOWN

You know, O Lord, that sometimes when I pray, a crowd of problems and worries rushes in upon me and disturbs my peace and my focus. Jesus, Prince of Peace, help me wrap all these concerns in a bundle and lay them quietly at your feet, then look into your face in hope and confidence and joyful rest. Praise be to you, Holy Savior. Amen.

❋ ❋ ❋

WHEN DISCOURAGED

O Lord, sometimes I am faint, or discouraged, or weak. Then you say to me, "Be strong, and let your heart take courage, all you who wait for the LORD" (Ps. 31:24). And so I draw strength from you and trust in your Spirit, your Word, your everlasting love, and your remembered promises. I worship you this day, loving Lord. Amen.

❋ ❋ ❋

WHEN I HAVE SINNED OR SENSE CONVICTION OF SIN

O God, I frankly confess that I have again failed you in ways I have done before. I deeply repent. Forgive and restore me, O Lord, and touch me deeply by your healing Spirit, that I may depend every moment on your sustaining grace and exercise all my powers to serve you and your mission. This I pray in full confidence in your power, grace, and loving goodwill. Amen.

❋ ❋ ❋

WHEN DOUBTS ASSAIL

O Lord, fortify my faith. Sometimes I feel full of doubts, or assailed by questions. Yet I trust in you. To whom else shall I go? My hope and rest are in you. Glory to you, Lord, Savior, and Healer. Amen.

ADDITIONAL PRAYERS FOR WORSHIP AND MEDITATION

PRAYER 1

"All Thy works with joy surround Thee . . ." Lord help me today by your Spirit to join all your works in joyfully praising you for who you are and what you are doing and promise, I pray. Amen.

> All Thy works with joy surround Thee,
> Earth and heav'n reflect Thy rays,
> Stars and angels sing around Thee,
> Center of unbroken praise.
> Field and forest, vale and mountain,
> Flow'ry meadow, flashing sea,
> Singing bird and flowing fountain
> Call us to rejoice in Thee.
> —Henry J. van Dyke, 1907

※ ※ ※

PRAYER 2

"Breathe on me, Breath of God." Holy Spirit, awaken within me a deeper holy hunger to know you in all your fullness. Blessed Jesus, live and act in my life this day, I pray, that I may perfectly love you and know deep communion with you in all I do. Amen.

> Breathe on me, Breath of God.
> Fill me with life anew,
> That I may love what Thou dost love,
> And do what Thou wouldst do.
> —Edwin Hatch, 1878

❋ ❋ ❋

PRAYER 3

Holy Lord, I seek to walk in communion with you today—Father, Son, and Spirit. I pray that by the infusion of your Spirit, and through my respiration in your Spirit, I would live and act so that people would see Jesus. Amen.

> Make a joyful noise to the LORD, all the earth.
>> Worship the LORD with gladness;
>> come into his presence with singing.
>
> Know that the LORD is God.
>> It is he that made us, and we are his;
>> we are his people, and the sheep of his pasture.

> —Psalm 100:1–3

❋ ❋ ❋

PRAYER 4

Lord Jesus, I bow humbly in your presence at the start of a new day. I thank you that you are here, and that you promise to be with me through all the hours ahead. I worship you now and ask that all my life today may be lived in worship to you. Amen.

Enter his gates with thanksgiving,
and his courts with praise.
Give thanks to him, bless his name.

For the LORD is good;
his steadfast love endures forever,
and his faithfulness to all generations.

—Psalm 100:4–5

❄ ❄ ❄

PRAYER 5

Holy Father, by your own Spirit, give me today the compassion and resilience and vision of the mind of Christ, I pray as I worship you now. Amen.

Hear my prayer, O LORD; let my cry come to you.
Do not hide your face from me in the day of my distress.
Incline your ear to me; answer me speedily in the day when I call.

—Psalm 102:1–2

❄ ❄ ❄

PRAYER 6

Lord of love, justice, and peace, I rest softly in your presence. Praise to you, Father, Son, and Holy Spirit. Help me walk joyfully in the freedom of healthy disciplines today as I seek to honor you, I pray. Amen.

Bless the LORD, O my soul,
and all that is within me, bless his holy name.
Bless the LORD, O my soul, and do not forget all his benefits—
who forgives all your iniquity, who heals all your diseases,
who redeems your life from the Pit,
who crowns you with steadfast love and mercy,
who satisfies you with good as long as you live
so that your youth is renewed like the eagle's.

—Psalm 103:1–5

❄ ❄ ❄

PRAYING WITH HABAKKUK

Eternal God, who often tarries beyond the time we hope for, but not beyond the time you have appointed; from whom come in due season the truth that cannot lie, the counsel that cannot fail: make us faithful to stand upon your watchtower, and to wait for what you will say to us; that by our faith we may live, and at the last behold your righteousness prevail; to the glory of your name.

—Based on Habakkuk; from *Daily Prayer*

❋ ❋ ❋

FOR THE BEAUTY OF THE EARTH

We give you thanks, most gracious God, for the beauty of earth and sky and sea; for the richness of mountains, plains, and rivers; for the songs of birds and the loveliness of flowers. We praise you for these good gifts, and pray that we may safeguard them for our posterity. Grant that we may continue to grow in our grateful enjoyment of your abundant creation, to the honor and glory of your name, now and for ever. *Amen.*

—*The Book of Common Prayer*

❋ ❋ ❋

FOR THE DIVERSITY OF RACES AND CULTURES

O God, who created all peoples in your image, we thank you for the wonderful diversity of races and cultures in this world. Enrich our lives by ever-widening circles of fellowship, and show us your presence in those who differ most from us, until our knowledge of your love is made perfect in our love for all your children; through Jesus Christ our Lord. *Amen.*

—*The Book of Common Prayer*